Yale University and New Haven

Bruce Ink

Contents

Legend

★★★ **Highly recommended**
★★ **Recommended**
★ **Interesting**

Sight symbols

Walking tour with departure point and direction

- Visitor Information
- Church
- B — Letter locating a sight
- ▪ ▲ — Other points of interest
- ▪ — Statue, monument
- Panorama – View
- Building described
- Other Yale University building
- Yale-owned lease buildings
- Other buildings
- University campus grounds
- Fountain

All maps are oriented north, unless otherwise indicated by a directional arrow.

Other symbols

- 94 — Interstate Highway
- 44 — US Highway
- 25 — Other Route
- Highway, interchange
- Toll road
- Divided highway
- Major, minor route
- Ferry
- Airport
- Parking
- Post office
- Hospital
- City street with median
- Pedestrian walkways
- Digression

About this Guide

Within each entry, **Times and Charges** (including addresses, telephone numbers, visiting hours and admission charges) appear in *italics* or in blue. New Haven offers **digressions**–places where one can take a break during the visit–identified on the maps with the symbol ●. The guide also includes symbols for parking 🅿, wheelchair accessibility ♿, and on-site eating facilities ✗. Letters in brackets, such as **[BX]**, indicate the coordinates for principal sights on the maps.

Michelin Travel Publications wishes to acknowledge the Yale University Tercentennial Planning Committee for their role in the development of this guide and additionally **Judith Ann Schiff**, Chief Research Archivist, Manuscripts and Archives, Sterling Memorial Library, for her contributions.

Michael Marsland /Yale University

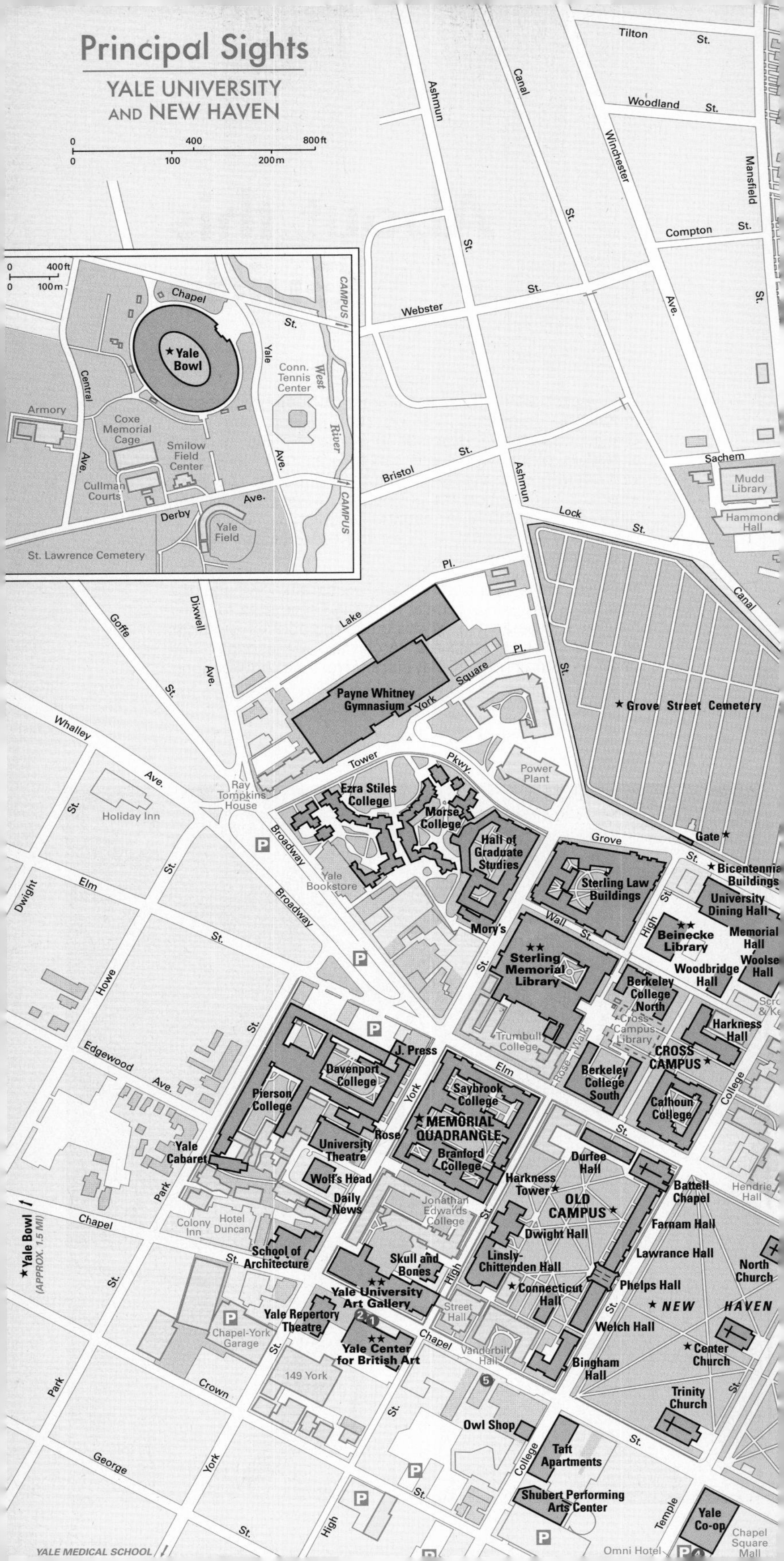

Principal Sights
YALE UNIVERSITY AND NEW HAVEN
0 400 800 ft
0 100 200 m
Yale Bowl
Chapel St.
Yale Ave.
Central Ave.
Armory
Coxe Memorial Cage
Smilow Field Center
Conn. Tennis Center
West River
Cullman Courts
Derby Ave.
Yale Field
St. Lawrence Cemetery
CAMPUS
Tilton St.
Woodland St.
Mansfield St.
Compton St.
Winchester Ave.
Canal St.
Ashmun St.
Webster St.
Bristol St.
Sachem
Mudd Library
Hammond Hall
Lock St.
Lake Pl.
Goffe St.
Dixwell Ave.
Whalley Ave.
York Square Pl.
Payne Whitney Gymnasium
Tower Pkwy.
Power Plant
Grove Street Cemetery
Ezra Stiles College
Morse College
Hall of Graduate Studies
Ray Tompkins House
Holiday Inn
Broadway
Grove St.
Gate
Bicentennial Buildings
Sterling Law Buildings
University Dining Hall
Memorial Hall
Woolsey Hall
Yale Bookstore
Mory's
Wall St.
High St.
Beinecke Library
Sterling Memorial Library
Woodbridge Hall
Berkeley College North
Dwight St.
Elm St.
Howe St.
Trumbull College
Cross Campus Library
Harkness Hall
CROSS CAMPUS
Edgewood Ave.
J. Press
Davenport College
Pierson College
Rose Walk
Berkeley College South
Calhoun College
College St.
Saybrook College
MEMORIAL QUADRANGLE
Branford College
Yale Cabaret
University Theatre
Wolf's Head
Daily News
Durfee Hall
Battell Chapel
Hendrie Hall
Harkness Tower
OLD CAMPUS
Jonathan Edwards College
Dwight Hall
Farnam Hall
Lawrance Hall
Park St.
Chapel St.
Colony Inn
Hotel Duncan
School of Architecture
Skull and Bones
Linsly-Chittenden Hall
North Church
Yale University Art Gallery
Connecticut Hall
Phelps Hall
NEW HAVEN
Yale Repertory Theatre
Street Hall
Welch Hall
Chapel-York Garage
Yale Center for British Art
Vanderbilt Hall
Bingham Hall
Center Church
149 York
Crown St.
Trinity Church
Owl Shop
Taft Apartments
George St.
York St.
Shubert Performing Arts Center
Temple St.
Yale Co-op
Chapel Square Mall
Omni Hotel
YALE MEDICAL SCHOOL
Yale Bowl (APPROX. 1.5 MI)

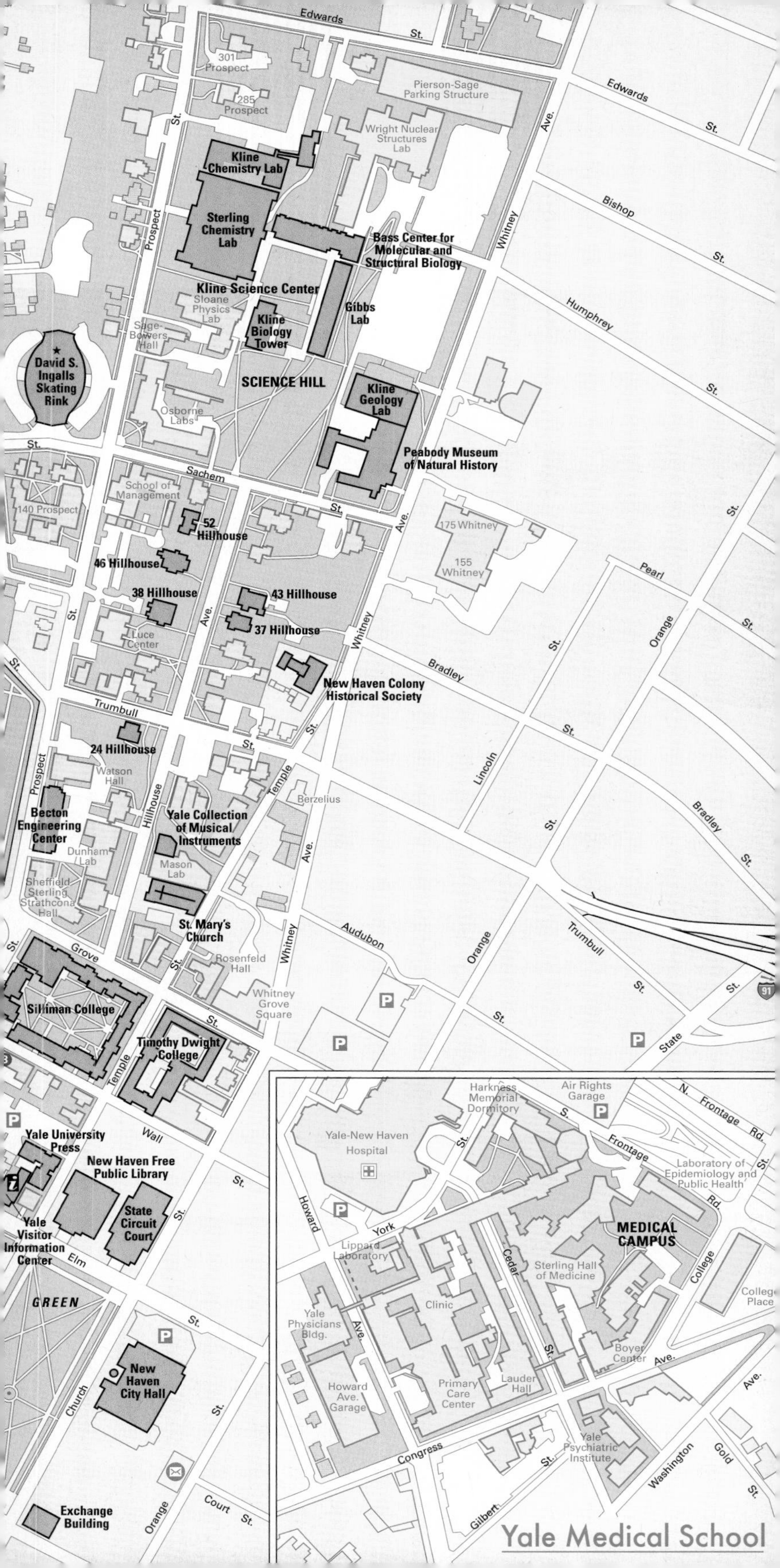
Edwards St.
301 Prospect
285 Prospect
Pierson-Sage Parking Structure
Wright Nuclear Structures Lab
Kline Chemistry Lab
Sterling Chemistry Lab
Bass Center for Molecular and Structural Biology
Kline Science Center
Sloane Physics Lab
Kline Biology Tower
Gibbs Lab
Sage-Bowers Hall
David S. Ingalls Skating Rink
SCIENCE HILL
Osborne Labs
Kline Geology Lab
Peabody Museum of Natural History
Prospect St.
Whitney Ave.
Bishop St.
Humphrey St.
Sachem St.
School of Management
140 Prospect
52 Hillhouse
46 Hillhouse
38 Hillhouse
43 Hillhouse
37 Hillhouse
Luce Center
175 Whitney
155 Whitney
Pearl St.
Orange St.
Bradley St.
New Haven Colony Historical Society
Trumbull St.
24 Hillhouse
Watson Hall
Becton Engineering Center
Yale Collection of Musical Instruments
Dunham Lab
Mason Lab
Sheffield Sterling Strathcona Hall
St. Mary's Church
Temple St.
Berzelius
Lincoln St.
Hillhouse Ave.
Audubon St.
Rosenfeld Hall
Whitney Grove Square
Grove St.
Silliman College
Timothy Dwight College
State St.
91
Wall St.
Yale University Press
New Haven Free Public Library
State Circuit Court
Yale Visitor Information Center
Elm St.
GREEN
New Haven City Hall
Church St.
Orange St.
Court St.
Exchange Building
Harkness Memorial Dormitory
Air Rights Garage
N. Frontage Rd.
S. Frontage Rd.
Yale-New Haven Hospital
Laboratory of Epidemiology and Public Health
Howard Ave.
York St.
MEDICAL CAMPUS
Lippard Laboratory
Cedar St.
Sterling Hall of Medicine
College St.
College Place
Clinic
Yale Physicians Bldg.
Boyer Center
Howard Ave. Garage
Primary Care Center
Lauder Hall
Yale Psychiatric Institute
Congress Ave.
Washington Ave.
Gold St.
Gilbert St.
Yale Medical School

Michael Marsland / Yale University

Introduction

Time Line

The Rise and Fall of the New Haven Colony

In 1637 two devout English Puritans, the Rev. John Davenport and his friend Theophilus Eaton, a wealthy merchant, led two shiploads of 500 followers to settle in America. It was Davenport's mission to found "an independent kingdom of Christ" and a college to educate its leaders. Landing first in Boston, Eaton explored and selected for their settlement the large harbor and rich meadows of Quinnipiack. Mostly Londoners and well to do, the settlers preferred trade to farming. The New Haven Colony did not prosper though as there was little to trade. Fur pelts and minerals were scarce, and agriculture was poorly managed. Then by the middle of the century, the Puritans took control of England's government, and some settlers returned home. Of those who remained many expressed dissatisfaction with the authoritarian leadership of the elite few who governed the theocracy. To repress dissent Governor Eaton's "Blue Laws" became even stricter, forbidding dancing, card playing, the celebration of Christmas, and most activities except prayer on the Sabbath. After the Restoration of the English monarchy in 1660, New Haven's independent status eroded. A new royal charter defined New Haven as part of the colony of Connecticut, and one by one the colony towns of Branford, Guilford, Milford, Stamford (including Greenwich), and Southold, Long Island, seceded and joined Connecticut. On January 7, 1665, New Haven finally united with Connecticut. With his dream to found a college in New Haven shattered, Davenport moved to Boston in despair two years later.

1614 | Dutch explorer Adriaen Block visits Quinnipiack (New Haven) and names it Roodeberg (red mountain).

1615-49 | Reign of King Charles I of Great Britain.

1620 | The Pilgrims arrive on the Mayflower and establish Plymouth Colony.

1637 | **Theophilus Eaton** and **John Davenport** sail from England to Boston with 500 Puritan colonists.

1638 | Puritan colonists sail from Boston and settle in Quinnipiack. Town laid out in plan of nine squares.

1640 | Quinnipiack settlement renamed New Haven.

1643 | Formation of the New Haven Colony; Eaton chosen governor.

1649 | Execution of King Charles I of Great Britain.

1650 | Governor Eaton's "Blue Laws" regulating public and private conduct adopted.

1660 | The Restoration and accession of Charles II.

1661 | Two regicides, signers of death warrant of Charles I, flee England. They are sheltered in New Haven and hidden in Judges Cave.

1665 | New Haven Colony unites with the Colony of Connecticut.

Colonial Yale and New Haven

Through the rest of the 17C, New Haven remained largely an agricultural town, with its spacious Green, or marketplace, at the center. In 1701 Davenport's successor as minister, **James Pierpont**, convinced that the church was in decline and could be restored only with the creation of a college to provide an educated clergy and civic leaders, organized a group of Connecticut ministers to meet and plan for its establishment. In the same year, New Haven, already a county seat, was designated a co-capital of the colony with Hartford. When the governor and General Assembly met in New Haven for the first time in October, they passed "An Act for Liberty to Erect a Collegiate School." The new trustees then selected Saybrook at the mouth of the Connecticut River as a more convenient site for the school, but over time the location proved an unpopular choice, and in 1716 they voted to move it to New Haven. The completion of a college building facing the Green was made possible by donations from residents and an Englishman named **Elihu Yale**. Yale's father, a stepson of Governor Eaton, had returned to England with his family, but his brother and other kinsmen had remained in the area. After receiving donations of goods sold for £500 and books from Elihu Yale, in 1718 the school was renamed Yale College. By the middle of the 18C, the local economy began to thrive as shipping increased. A fine brick structure, Connecticut Hall, the oldest standing Yale and New Haven building, replaced the old wooden hall. By 1775 town and gown were fully committed to achieving independence from England and fortunately had to defend the town only once when British forces briefly occupied and plundered it in 1779. After the war, New Haven planned for a new era by obtaining a city charter, divesting itself of its surrounding agricultural towns, and concentrating on its commercial development.

1701 The Collegiate School, later named Yale, is founded by 10 Connecticut ministers meeting in nearby Branford.
New Haven is designated co-capital, with Hartford, of the Colony of Connecticut.

1716 Yale trustees vote to move the school from Saybrook to New Haven "as a very Convenient place for it, and for which the Most Liberal Donations are given."

1717 Statehouse erected on Upper Green.

1718 The Collegiate School is named **Yale College** in honor of Elihu Yale's donations.
Yale student enrollment reaches 37.

Manuscripts and Archives / Yale University

Elihu Yale

1750 Construction of **Connecticut Hall** on the Old Campus, the oldest standing building in New Haven.

1759 First public planting of elm trees, leading to later nickname of New Haven as the "Elm City."

1761 New Haven town population reaches approximately 6,000, about 1,500 in present city area.

1775 Outbreak of the American Revolution.
Captain Benedict Arnold of New Haven and his company march off to join the Continental Army in Massachusetts.

5 Jul. 1779 British troops capture and briefly occupy New Haven, defended by Yale and town militia.

1783 End of the American Revolution; Britain recognizes the independence of the 13 colonies.

1784 Incorporation of the City of New Haven. Roger Sherman, the only signer of all four major documents of American democracy, elected mayor.
New Haven population hits 3,500. Yale student enrollment reaches 252.

1789 George Washington is chosen first president of the US.
The French Revolution begins.

1793 Artist **John Trumbull's** campus plan for Yale's **Old Brick Row** adopted.

1797 Establishment of the **Grove Street Cemetery**, the first chartered burial ground in the US, and the first to be regularly laid out with family and institutional lots.

Arts and Sciences Flourish in the Elm City

Eli Whitney's invention of the cotton gin, shortly after his graduation from Yale in 1792, transformed the Southern economy, but copyright infringements made it unprofitable for him. He then turned his ingenuity to the manufacture of guns that were to be assembled for the first time using calibrated interchangeable parts. In 1798, at the northern outskirts of New Haven on Whitney Avenue he built Whitneyville, the country's first factory village, where he proceeded to fill the first major US government arms contract for ten thousand muskets and bayonets. Whitney's production plan known as "the American System," was the prototype of modern manufacturing in New Haven and elsewhere.

Yale's president Timothy Dwight advanced the sciences in America by appointing Benjamin Silliman the first science professor in America in 1802. Over the next 50 years Silliman developed both the arts and sciences, forming the first graduate school and a separate scientific school at Yale. He brought the fine arts to academia and the city by arranging for John Trumbull's paintings to be given to Yale and housed in the first university art gallery in 1832. In the late 1860s, the first university art school was opened with a do-

Manuscripts and Archives/Yale University

nation from a New Haven alumnus and his wife, who specified that the school be coed. Many New Haven women attended Yale's first coed school. Local artists included George Durrie, whose depictions of country scenes around New Haven popularized in Currier & Ives prints are still familiar images on Christmas cards. The artists John Trumbull and Samuel Morse (Class of 1810) lived at times in New Haven and helped to encourage patronage of the art gallery. Large crowds came to view its new collections of Early Italian and American paintings. In the 1870s the Peabody Museum opened to showcase the dinosaur and other bones and fossils collected by Professor O.C. Marsh and his "bonediggers" on Western expeditions. Architecture flourished with the support of a growing class of wealthy merchants, manufacturers, and entrepreneurs who built mansions in the latest Greek Revival, Italianate and Gothic Victorian styles, first facing the Green on Elm Street, known as Quality Row, then around Wooster Square, and especially on Hillhouse Avenue dubbed by Charles Dickens, "the most beautiful street in America." Local inventions and improvements made New Haven a national center for the manufacture of hardware, carriages, corsets, rifles, and rubber footwear; and thousands of skilled and unskilled workers, men and women, were needed to fill its factories.

1798	**Eli Whitney**, Yale Class of 1792, establishes a gun factory in New Haven, the first factory to utilize a system of interchangeable parts, known as the American System.
1799	Connecticut Academy of Arts and Sciences, one of the oldest scientific societies, is founded in New Haven.
1800	New Haven population reaches 5,000. Yale enrollment is 217.
1802	**Benjamin Silliman** is appointed first science professor at Yale and in the US.
1810	**James Brewster** opens a carriage factory, leading to the development of New Haven as the center of fine carriage manufacture in America.
1812-14	War of 1812.
1812-15	Building of the three present-day church structures on the New Haven Green.
1813	Organization of Yale's medical school.
1815	Beginning of steamboat services between New Haven and New York.
1818	Professor Benjamin Silliman begins publication of *The American Journal of Science*, one of the world's great scientific journals, still published in New Haven.
1823	Statement of Faith for University Faculty and Officers abolished.
1824	Construction of Farmington Canal begins.
1830	New Haven population reaches 10,000. Yale enrollment is 502.
1832	**The Trumbull Gallery** opens, the first art museum connected with a university in the US.
1836	**Samuel Colt** invents the automatic revolver in the Whitney Arms Co.
1839	Railroad line opens from New Haven to Meriden, Connecticut.
1839-41	Yale and New Haven community work together to secure the freedom of the **Amistad Captives**, a landmark event in American history.
1843	The L. Candee Co. begins to manufacture rubber footware, licensing New Havener Charles Goodyear's vulcanization patents. First collegiate rowing races are held in New Haven harbor.
1845	Potato famine in Ireland starts large wave of immigration to New Haven.
1850	New Haven population is 20,345. Yale enrollment reaches 555.
1853	Alexander C. Twining, a New Haven engineer, invents the first artificial ice machine, and by 1855 the ice trade is thriving in New Haven.
1854	Seneca Oil Co. organizes in New Haven and successfully drills the world's first oil well in Pennsylvania.
1858	Modern highway construction is enabled by the invention of the rock crusher by **Eli Whitney Blake**, Eli Whitney's nephew.
1860	**Philos Blake**, Eli's brother, invents the corkscrew. New Haven population reaches 40,000. Yale enrollment is 649.
1861-65	Civil War.
1861	Yale awards first doctor of philosophy degrees in the US. First corset factory opens leading to New Haven's becoming the largest center of corset making in the world.
14 Apr. 1865	John Wilkes Booth assassinates President Lincoln at Ford's Theatre in Washington, DC.
1867	**Oliver Winchester** establishes the Winchester Repeating Arms Co., manufacturer of the Winchester 73, "the gun that won the west."

1869 The **Yale School of the Fine Arts**, the first collegiate art school and Yale's first coed school, opens through gifts of New Haveners **Augustus** and **Caroline Street**.

1872 New Haven African American businesswoman **Mary Goodman** endows a scholarship fund for the education of African Americans in the Divinity School.

1873 New Haven ceases to be co-capital of Connecticut.

1876 New Haven native **Edward Bouchet** receives the degree of Doctor of Philosophy from Yale, the first doctorate awarded to an African American by an American university.

1878 World's first telephone switchboard and telephone exchange open in New Haven.
First edition of the *Yale Daily News*.

The Changing College and City

From about 1880 Yale and New Haven entered an era of dramatic transition. The dominance of Congregationalists of English extraction in the city slipped away as large numbers of immigrants moved in. Mostly from Eastern and Southern Europe, they were predominately Italians and Russian Jews. The Irish population dating from the building of the Farmington Canal had burgeoned after the potato famine and continued to grow. So many Italians came to work in the Sargent Hardware Factory that New Haven was said to have the largest percentage of Italians outside their homeland. At the turn of the century an Italian consular office was opened on Wooster Square, the heart of the new Italian neighborhood.

Yale grew and became more cosmopolitan as increasing numbers of its students were selected from the most prestigious prep schools. Its great teachers and researchers earned international reputations, such as **William Graham Sumner**, the first sociologist, and **William Lyon Phelps**, the first teacher of modern literature. In contrast, the students became more content to earn a gentleman's C, follow the new sports of football and rowing, and socialize in their fraternities and senior societies. The Old Brick Row was obscured by the construction of large stone dormitories that seemed to form a fortress separating the school from the city. Extending architecturally into the city, Yale built, and later replaced, elegant new schools and halls, including the Divinity School, the Berkeley Oval, and the Old Peabody Museum.

The density of the city's population led to the rise of slums and pollution that could not be stemmed by the City Beautiful reform movement in the early 20C. During this time Yale and New Haven grew apart physically and socially. After World War I, town-gown relations sank to a low point in May 1919, when newly returned veterans paraded past the campus and insults were exchanged about the contribution by each group to the war effort. Continuing animosity led to a march on Yale by 300 veterans and 5,000 residents and two days of rioting and violence that was finally quelled by armed state guardsmen. It was time for civic and educational reform.

Manuscripts and Archives/Yale University

1879 Yale football team. Captain Walter Camp holding the ball.

1880	New Haven population reaches 62,882. Yale enrollment climbs to 1,037.
1880-83	**Walter Camp**, as Yale student and coach, develops the game of American **football**, first played in New Haven.
1881	Italian, Jewish and Eastern European immigrants begin to settle in New Haven in large numbers.
1882	**Knights of Columbus**, an international fraternal and benevolent organization of Roman Catholic men, is founded in New Haven.
1889	Old Statehouse razed from the Green.
1892	**Lollipop** invented by the Bradley Smith Candy Co. of New Haven.
1895	**Louis' Lunch** serves the first **hamburger** sandwich (still being made in the traditional way). Founding of the New Haven Symphony Orchestra, the fourth oldest in the US.
1900	New Haven population reaches 108,000, 28 percent of whom are foreign born. Yale enrollment is 2,542.
1901	Woodbridge Hall, University Dining Hall, Woolsey Hall and Memorial Hall are constructed as Yale's Bicentennial Buildings.
1908	Founding of the *Yale University Press.*
1913	**A. C. Gilbert** ('09), inventor of scientific toys, introduces the Erector Set, his famous metal construction set, manufactured in New Haven, at the New York Toy Fair. After his defeat in 1912, President **William Howard Taft** becomes professor of constitutional law at Yale, living in New Haven until 1921 when he was appointed Chief Justice of the United States Supreme Court.
1914-18	World War I.
1914	Yale Bowl completed, the largest amphitheater to be constructed since the Roman Colosseum. Shubert Theatre opens and becomes famous for pre-Broadway openings of hit plays and musicals.
1918	Bequest of **John William Sterling** (Class of 1864) funds the construction of new buildings for the library, and graduate and professional schools of the university, and endows many professorships.

Restructuring and Redevelopment

As World War I alumni veterans debated the banning of the Yale alma mater, "Bright College Years," whose tune was a patriotic German song, its immortal closing line, "For God, for Country, and for Yale," was being carved into the archway of the majestic new Memorial Quadrangle. Looming above it was Harkness Tower, the world's tallest freestanding tower and the city's tallest landmark. A large bequest from John W. Sterling and donations from the Harkness family enabled the university to reform its educational system and build residential colleges, graduate and professional schools, and libraries to strengthen and broaden its educational mission. For the city Yale provided an excellent avenue of upward mobility as the tuition remained low and local students could live at home. Economically, the effects of the Great Depression on the city were mitigated by the university's ongoing rebuilding program, so extensive that it led to the toast, "Here's to Good Old Yale, Tear Her Down, Tear Her Down." During World War II the Yale campus was transformed into a military base where 20,000 men and women were trained for all areas of war service. Home front hardships were alleviated by the presence of Glenn Miller's air force band that marched to the Green and broadcast weekly from Yale's Woolsey Hall. War work carried New Haven through the late 1930s and 40s. Thereafter the changing economy and the exodus to the suburbs left the city in a depressed condition. New hope came to the city with the election of Mayor Richard C. Lee in 1954 who successfully tapped federal funds and, with the advice of Yale experts in planning and architecture, undertook a major redevelopment program. At the same time, Yale president **A. Whitney Griswold** redefined the liberal arts educational mission of Yale and enlivened the architectural appearance of the university by inviting the best modern architects to design its buildings. Redevelopment did not solve New Haven's problems however, and by 1970 the population had slipped from a plateau of over 160,000 to 137,000. During the civil rights era of the late 1960s and early 70s student protests, boycotts relating to the Black Panther Trials in New Haven, and strikes of Yale's unionized workers tested town-gown relations. Then discussion over the site planning of the Yale Center for British Art in downtown retail space led to an innovative new perspective in planning, compromise and preservation. Yale and the city continued to work cooperatively in developing mutually beneficial projects. The university is now New Haven's largest employer with over 10,000 faculty, professionals, and staff, about the same size as its student body. In 1997 Yale appointed the first vice president for New Haven and State Affairs in recognition of the priority of the university's relations with the city and region.

Michael Marsland/Yale University

Harkness Tower

1920	Completion of Yale-New Haven landmark **Harkness Tower**, at the time the tallest freestanding tower in the US.
1926	End of compulsory daily chapel for Yale students.
1929	Stock market crash.
1930	Sterling Memorial Library completed.
1932	Payne Whitney Gymnasium, "The Cathedral of Sweat," completed.
1933	Opening of the Yale undergraduate residential colleges, under the college plan funded by **Edward S. Harkness**.
1939-45	World War II.
1942	Conversion of Yale campus into wartime training school.
1943	**Captain Glenn Miller** forms Army Air Forces "Superband" at Yale, broadcasting weekly from the campus.
1954	City Redevelopment program instituted under Mayor **Richard C. Lee**.
22 Nov. 1963	President Kennedy is assassinated in Dallas, Texas.
1963	Completion of Beinecke Library.
1969	**Coeducation** of Yale College.
1977	Opening of Yale Center for British Art.
1990	Audubon Arts Center is completed. Yale begins largest construction and renovation project since the 1920s.
1992	Unveiling of the Amistad Memorial in front of New Haven city hall.
1993	Installation of the Women's Table by **Maya Lin**.
1995	Special Olympics World Games held in New Haven. Opening of Henry R. Luce Hall, home of Yale Center for International and Area Studies.
1998	New Haven population is 123,000. Yale enrollment reaches 10,990.
Aug. 2000	New Haven becomes the official home port of the freedom schooner *Amistad*.
2001	Yale Tercentennial.

Hotels

The Night Café (1888) by Vincent van Gogh

Restaurants

Nightlife

ew Haven

a limited range of accommodation alternatives – elegant and breakfasts, modern and high-tech hotels to run-of-the mill s found mostly outside the city core and in the suburbs. Rates r on weekends. Amenities include television, restaurant, and oking rooms. The more expensive hotels also offer workout service and valet service. Downtown hotels may charge a fee

rowed down the list to those that offer the best accommodation for the ... ion, comfort, and the price. We have also included 800 numbers for chain accommodations in the surrounding area.

All venues are in New Haven. Rates are for a standard room, double occupancy in high season; prices are indicated in US dollars.

$$$	$150-$225
$$	$75-$150
$	under $75

Colony Inn – *1157 Chapel St.* *203-776-1234 or 800-458-8810. Fax 203-772-3929. www.ColonyatYale.com.* **$$** Located downtown, this cozy hotel is conveniently close to campus, shopping and entertainment. 86 rooms.

Grand Chalet Inn & Suites – *400 Sargent Dr.* *203-562-1111 or 800-524-2538. Fax 203-865-7440. www.sussechalet.com.* **$$** This recently renovated all-suite hotel affords views of New Haven harbor. 158 rooms.

Holiday Inn at Yale – *30 Whalley Ave.* *203-777-6221 or 800-465-4329. Fax 203-772-1089. www.holiday-inn.com.* **$$** Reasonable prices and close proximity to the Yale campus and theaters make this chain hotel a favorite of campus visitors.

Hotel Duncan – *1151 Chapel St.* *203-787-1273. Fax 203-787-0160.* **$** Step back in time to one of New Haven's oldest hotels. Modern conveniences aren't a priority, but its great location and unassuming staff make for an enjoyable stay. 90 rooms.

New Haven Hotel – *229 George St.* *203-498-3100 or 800-644-6835. Fax 203-498-0911. www.newhavenhotel.com.* **$$** Well-appointed rooms and friendly service characterize this downtown hotel. 92 rooms.

Omni New Haven Hotel at Yale – *155 Temple St.* *203-772-6664 or 800-843-6664. Fax 203-974-6777. www.omnihotels.com.* **$$$** This upscale property is conveniently located next to campus and is New Haven's premier business hotel. Its rooftop restaurant provides great views of downtown New Haven and the harbor. 306 rooms.

Quality Inn and Conference Center – *100 Pond Lily Ave.* *203-387-6651 or 800-228-5151. Fax 203-387-6651. www.schafferhotels.com.* **$$** Clean, comfortable and reasonable, this hotel is a favorite for conference-goers. 123 rooms.

Residence Inn by Marriott – *3 Long Wharf Dr.* *203-777-5337. www.residenceinn.com. Fax 203-777-2808.* **$$** An all-suite hotel, rooms have sitting areas and fully equipped kitchens. 112 suites.

Bed and Breakfast Inns

The Historic Mansion Inn – *600 Chapel St.* *203-865-8324 or 888-512-6278. Fax 203-787-0059. www.thehistoricmansioninn.com.* **$$** Marble fireplaces and well-appointed rooms await you at this recently renovated 19C Greek Revival home. 10 rooms.

The Inn at Oyster Point – *104 Howard Ave.* *203-773-3334. Fax 203-777-4150.* **$$** Enjoy a taste of Old New England at the historic harbor district in one of the inn's rooms or fully-equipped suites. 3 rooms, 3 suites.

Swan Cove Bed & Breakfast – *115 Sea St.* *203-776-3240 or toll free 877-499-8165. Fax 203-776-8649. www.swancove.com.* **$$** Located away from downtown New Haven, this intimate Queen Anne house offers cozy rooms with antique furnishings. 5 rooms, 2 suites.

Three Chimneys Inn – *1201 Chapel St.* *203-789-1201 or 800-443-1554. Fax 203-776-7363. www.threechimneysinn.com.* **$$$** Pamper yourself with a few nights at this elegant and completely modern 1847 mansion. 11 rooms.

Touch of Ireland – *670 Whitney Ave.* *203-787-7997. Fax 203-787-7999.* **$$**. Conveniently located in East Rock on the edge of Yale's campus, this newly-renovated 1920s Colonial invites you to relax in the sun room or take the chill off a cold winter night next to the fireplace. 3 rooms.

Surrounding Area Hotels and Motels

Major hotel chains with locations in the New Haven area include:

	☎		☎
Best Western	800-528-1234	**Howard Johnson**	800-446-4656
Courtyard by Marriot	800-321-2211	**ITT Sheraton**	800-325-3535
Hampton Inn	800-426-7866	**Marriott**	800-228-9290
Hilton	800-445-8667	**Radisson**	800-333-3333
Holiday Inn	800-465-4329	**Ramada**	800-228-2828

Restaurant Haven

Hungry visitors to New Haven will be thrilled with the city's abundance of good restaurants at reasonable prices. With a particular emphasis on Italian, especially New Haven's famous pizza (Pepe's or Sally's?—we wouldn't dare), the city offers a great variety of cuisines. The list below represents a sampling of the city's well-frequented and popular eating establishments. Most restaurants are open daily and accept major credit cards. Prices indicate the average cost of an entree, an appetizer or dessert, and a beverage for one person (not including tax and tip, or alcoholic beverages).

$$$ = expensive ($25+)
$$ = moderate ($16-$24)
$ = inexpensive (under $15)

African/Ethiopian

Caffé Adulis
228 College St. ☎ *203-777-5081* $

Lalibela
176 Temple St. ☎ *203-789-1232* $

American

Archie Moore's
188 1/2 Willow St. ☎ *203-773-9870* $

BRU RM At Bar
254 Crown St. ☎ *203-495-8924* $

Copper Kitchen Restaurant
1008 Chapel St. ☎ *203-777-8010* $

Humphrey's East
175 Humphrey St. ☎ *203-782-1506* $

JP Dempsey's
974 State St. ☎ *203-624-5991* $

Kavanagh's
1166 Chapel St. ☎ *203-624-0520* $

Louis' Lunch
263 Crown St. ☎ *203-562-5507* $

Richter's Cafe
990 Chapel St. ☎ *203-777-0400* $

Tibwin Grill
220 College St. ☎ *203-624-1883* $$$

Zinc
964 Chapel St. ☎ *203-624-0507* $$

Continental

500 Blake Street Cafe
500 Blake St. ☎ *203-387-0500* $$

Christopher Martins
860 State St. ☎ *203-776-8835* $$

Cuban

Roomba
1044 Chapel St. ☎ *203-562-7666* $$

French

Union League Cafe
1032 Chapel St. ☎ *203-562-4299* $$$

Indian

India Palace
65 Howe St. ☎ *203-776-9010* $

Royal India
140 Howe St. ☎ *203-787-9493* $

Irish

Anna Liffey's Irish Pub & Restaurant
17 Whitney Ave. ☎ *203-773-1776* $

Italian

Consiglio's Restaurant
165 Wooster St. ☎ *203-865-4889* $$

Frank Pepe Pizzeria Napoletana, Inc.
157 Wooster St. ☎ *203-865-5762* $

Hot Tomato's
261 College St. ☎ *203-624-6331* $$

Modern Apizza
874 State St. ☎ *203-776-5306* $

Polo Grille & Wine Bar
7 Elm St. ☎ *203-787-9000* $$

Sally's Apizza
237 Wooster St. ☎ *203-624-5271* $

Scoozi Trattoria & Wine Bar
1104 Chapel St. ☎ *203-776-8268* $$

Tony & Lucille's Little Italy Restaurant
150 Wooster St. ☎ *203-787-1621* $

Tre Scalini Ristorante
100 Wooster St. ☎ *203-773-3373* $$

Yorkside Pizza
288 York St. ☎ *203-787-7471* $

Korean

Seoul Restaurant
343 Crown St. ☎ *203-497-9634* $

Malaysian

Bentara Restaurant
76 Orange St. ☎ *203-562-2511* $$

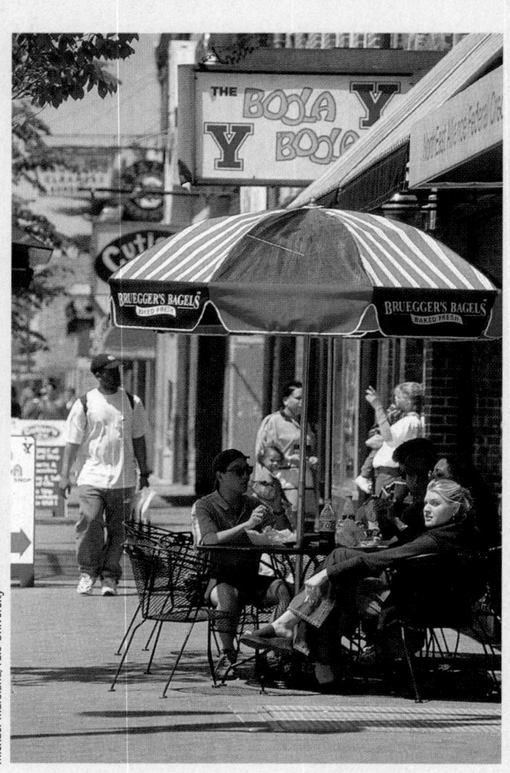

Michael Marsland/Yale University

Middle Eastern

Mamoun's Falafel Restaurant
85 Howe St. ☎ *203-562-*

Spanish

Café Pika Tapas
39 High St. ☎ *203-865-1*

Thai

Bangkok Garden Restaurant
172 York St. ☎ *203-789-86*

Indochine Pavilion
1180 Chapel St. ☎ *203-865-5033* $

Turkish

Istanbul Cafe
245 Crown St. ☎ *203-787-3881* $

Vegetarian

Claire's Corner Copia
1000 Chapel St. ☎ *203-562-3888* $

Nightlife

New Haven's nightlife is as diverse as its population with, of course, a special emphasis on college hangouts. Some establishments have a cover charge. Many restaurants become nightclubs in the evenings. Various bars and nightclubs serve food (menu may be scaled down to light appetizers after 10pm or 11pm). Because alcoholic beverages are served, proof of age is required to enter most nightclubs.

500 Blake St. *500 Blake St.*	☎ *203-387-0500*	Wed–Sat	Piano bar
Anna Liffey's Irish Pub & Restaurant *17 Whitney Ave.*	☎ *203-773-1776*	Mon	Irish music
Bar *254 Crown St.*	☎ *203-495-8924*	Tue, Fri-Sun	DJ Sun: Live acoustic
Cafe Nine *250 State St.*	☎ *203-789-8281* *http://over.to/cafenine*	Nightly	Live entertainment
Caffé Adulis *228 College St.*	☎ *203-777-5081*	Thur	Live jazz
Christopher Martin's *860 State St.*	☎ *203-776-8835*	Thur–Sat	Live music
Gotham Citi *130 Crown St.*	☎ *203-498-CITI*	Wed–Sat	Live, non-mainstream entertainment
GPSCY Bar Graduate & Professional Student Center at Yale *204 York St.* Open to the public	☎ *203-432-2638*	Nightly	On-campus bar with live music
Partners Cafe *365 Crown St.*	☎ *203-776-1014* *www.Partnerscafe.com*	Thur–Sat	DJ
Sports Haven *600 Long Wharf Dr.*	☎ *203-946-3201* *www.ctotb.com*	Daily	Simulcast action on jai-alai, racing and sports.
TK's American Café *285 George St.*	☎ *203-789-1776*	Sat	Live music
Toad's Place *300 York St.*	☎ *203-624-toad* *www.toadsplace.com*	Nightly	Live music
Tune Inn *29 Center St.*	☎ *203-772-4310* *www.elevatormusic.com*	Call	Live music

brought a Number of Books ...and laying them on the Table, words, or to this Effect: 'I give these books for founding a College olony.'"

First History of Yale, 1766

Starr Main Reference Room, Sterling Memorial Library

Yale University

Yale Today

Yale University is one of the most distinguished institutions of higher learning in the world. Today it is a private institution dedicated to the highest standards of teaching and research at the undergraduate and the graduate levels. Although it is not the largest Ivy League university, it is the only one with four professional schools in the arts.

Lay of the land – The main campus stretches about two miles from north to south on 225 acres and comprises two primary areas: central and medical. Although the campus is largely situated in the heart of an urban downtown, the city's Green and the university's open spaces and courtyards give it a small-town feeling. Three miles west of the campus are the principal outdoor athletic facilities, a golf course, and nature preserve, which bring the total acreage to 835—eight percent of New Haven's total area.

Organization – The university's 11,000 students, 3,200 faculty members, and staff of 7,000 are members of a diverse community. Among all students, women and men are represented in equal numbers. Its policy-making board, the Yale Corporation, has 19 members, two of whom are the governor and lieutenant governor of the State of Connecticut, a reflection of its state-chartered origins. A president serves as chief administrative officer, and a provost is the chief academic officer.

Academics – Yale College, the undergraduate school, is committed to a liberal arts education in which students, mostly 18 to 22 years old, explore a variety of fields and obtain a wide cultural background, which serves them well when they go into their professions. Bachelor of Arts, Bachelor of Liberal Studies, and Bachelor of Science degrees are awarded. The Graduate School of Arts and Sciences and the 10 professional schools—Architecture, Art, Divinity, Drama, Forestry and Environmental Studies, Law, Management, Medicine, Music, and Nursing—award master's, doctoral, and professional degrees for concentrated work in a field.

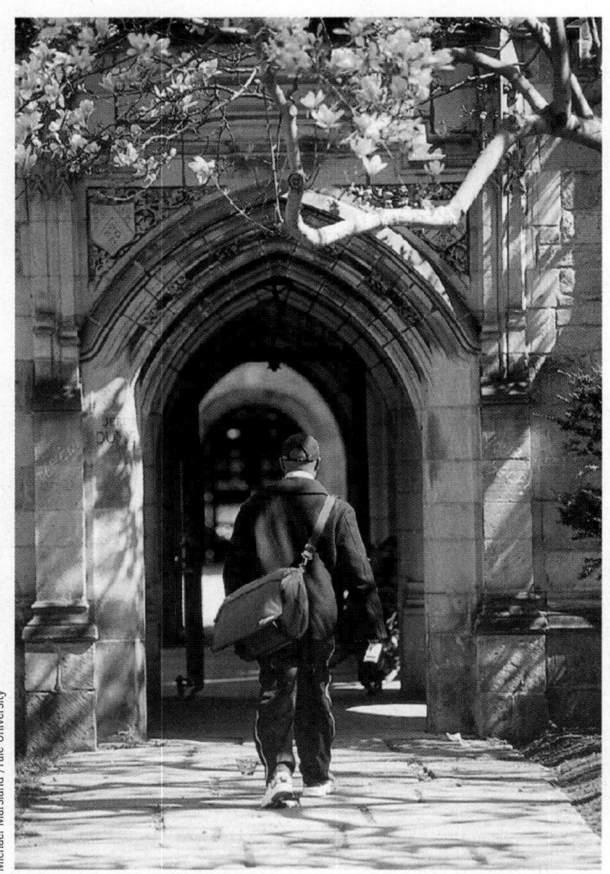

Michael Marsland /Yale University

Traditions

Alma mater, "Bright College Years" – "Bright College Years," the beloved alma mater of Yale College was written by Yale student Henry Durand in 1881, to the tune of the German patriotic song, "Die Wacht am Rhein." Sung at all football games, alumni events, and the concluding custom of the Class Day ceremony, it is traditional to wave a white handkerchief in the air during the song's last line, "For God, for Country, and for Yale!"

Class Day Pipes – The issuing of long white clay pipes to graduating seniors on Class Day is one of the few traditions to have endured from the earliest days of Yale College to the present. Soap bubbles may now rise from some bowls, but many students still observe the traditional tobacco ritual. In the 19C after smoking together the "pipes of peace," the seniors set them upright in the grass, and in a rush trampled upon and crushed them, so signifying the end of the pleasures of college life. Today it is customary to break the pipe and keep it as a memento.

Frisbee – The popular game and competitive sport of Frisbee originated at Yale in the early 20C. After consuming the popular pies made by the Frisbie Pie Company in nearby Bridgeport, students enjoyed tossing the empty pie tins. The baker's name pressed into the tin was shouted out to alert the catcher and bystanders, and the name of the game, then spelled Frisbie, stuck. In the 1950s, the Wham-O toy company started to market a plastic disc called the flying saucer. While conducting market research one of the owners saw Yale students playing and yelling "Frisbie." He liked the sound and renamed his toy, spelling it phonetically Frisbee.

"The Game" – To Yale and Harvard fans, The Game is the football match between arch rivals Yale and Harvard played since 1875. Except for the earliest years, it is the final game of the Yale football season held on the Saturday before Thanksgiving. The Game was cancelled nine times between 1877 and 1944 due to disagreements and wartimes, and postponed only once after news of President Kennedy's assassination reached the teams the day before the contest. The largest crowd to attend The Game in the Yale Bowl was 80,000 in 1920. As of 1999, Yale led the series with 62 wins, 45 losses and 8 ties.

Handsome Dan, the Yale Bulldog – The first and most famous of all college mascots is the Yale bulldog. In 1889, freshman Andrew B. Graves came upon a grimy bulldog in a New Haven blacksmith's shop. He could not resist the charms of the puppy he described as "a cross between an alligator and a horned toad" and bought him from the blacksmith for $65.00. A thorough scrubbing revealed a fine

Michael Marsland /Yale University

"Bright College Years"

white coat with brown head markings, and the delighted Andy named his bulldog Handsome Dan. Graves, a rower, took Dan with him everywhere including football and baseball games where he was an enthusiastic rooter. Dan emulated his master, barking whenever Yale scored. At football games he had to be kept on a stout leash. When ordered to speak to the enemy, Dan faced the rival stands with angry barks and savage growls, working himself into contortions of rage never before seen. It was said that the Harvard team for years owed its continued existence to the fact that the leather rope held. The burly bulldog was soon adopted as the official Yale mascot, a new word derived from the title of the French opera, *La Mascotte*, meaning a person, or a thing, animate or inanimate, supposed to bring luck. After Dan's death in 1897 his hide was stuffed and presented to the Yale trophy room. Today he sits jauntily posed in a sealed glass case in the Payne Whitney Gymnasium. Until the advent of Handsome Dan II in 1933, Dan I was the Yale icon immortalized in posters and pennants, and especially in song. In 1911, undergraduate Cole Porter honored Dan in the Yale fight song, "Bull-Dog! Bull-Dog! Bow, wow, wow." The current monarch of mascots is Handsome Dan XVI.

Ivy Planting and Ode – The planting of ivy by the graduating college class began in 1852, when it was included in the ceremony for Presentation Day, the forerunner of Class Day. Most of the plantings are around the Old Library, now Dwight Hall, and other Old Campus buildings, or in the Sterling Memorial Library courtyard, with the class year inscribed in the wall above. In the 1860s an Ivy Ode in Latin was added to the Class Day program. As Yale has become more multicultural, the odes are delivered in a variety of classical and contemporary languages that enliven and enrich the tradition.

Yale Blue – The selection of the college color, Yale blue, a dark blue (nearly navy) with a hint of purple, was not official until 1894. In the early 19C green was the favorite color associated with the college. As collegiate sports competition evolved beginning with Yale rowing in 1843, it became necessary to distinguish one team from another. The informal use of blue flags on Yale boats became fixed in 1852, in the first intercollegiate rowing contest against Harvard. Four decades later the Yale Corporation voted that "the shade of blue known as the color of the University of Oxford be officially adopted as the color of Yale University."

Yale Seal and Coat-of-Arms – The meaning of the Yale coat-of-arms seen in numerous campus carvings and publications has puzzled many with its Hebrew and Latin text. Its standard form depicts a Yale blue shield upon which rests an open book inscribed in Hebrew and a ribbon beneath the shield inscribed in Latin. Yale adopted the seal in the early 18C when students were required to study Latin and Hebrew. The book is identified as the Old Testament of the Bible by the words "Urim and Thummim," the names of sacred lots to be cast for the purpose of ascertaining the divine will. *Lux et Veritas*, the Latin text, is a translation from the Hebrew and means in English, "Light and Truth."

Student Life

The Residential College System – Undergraduate social life is organized mainly within the residential college system. Students are usually randomly assigned to one of the 12 colleges where they not only live and eat most of their meals, but also are part of a small, structured community. Each residential college has two major administrative officers: the Master, the chief officer responsible for the academic and social life of the residential college, and the Dean, the chief academic and personal adviser to the students. Student life is enriched by fellows, who are selected from a wide spectrum of Yale faculty, administrators and staff, and associate fellows, distinguished alumni and other individuals from the local community and all over the world. Each college has a library and a computer room and offers its own seminar courses that supplement the regular curriculum. Individual colleges also have unique programs and features including endowed lectureships, academic journals, printing presses, gyms, performance spaces, art galleries, and cafes. Inspired by the college system of Oxford and Cambridge, each Yale residential college has an affiliation with a college at Oxford or Cambridge. The several hundred students in each college organize their own dramatic, musical, and special interest clubs and intramural teams. Throughout the year, the community is welcome to attend the variety of plays and concerts produced by the colleges.

Michael Marsland/Yale University

Clubs and Organizations – Other student organizations are college wide in membership. Some of the oldest and best known are the musical groups, including the Yale Bands, Yale Glee Club, Yale Symphony Orchestra, the Yale Banjo and Mandolin Association dating back to 1885, and the Yale Guild of Carillonneurs, whose members play the Harkness Tower carillon twice daily. Also outstanding are the a cappella singing groups including the oldest traditional men's groups such as the Whiffenpoofs, Baker's Dozen, Duke's Men, and Spizzwinks. Since Yale went coed in 1969, women's groups were formed including the New Blue, Proof of the Pudding, and Something Extra. Coed groups such as Redhot & Blue, and Shades are also popular. The oldest of the drama groups is the Yale Dramatic Association, known as the Yale Dramat, founded in 1899. Some of its early famous alumni include Monty Woolley, Cole Porter, and Thornton Wilder.

The largest undergraduate organization is the Yale Political Union. Founded in 1934 to combat the political apathy of the 1930s and modeled after union groups at Oxford and Cambridge, it includes a spectrum of student political parties from Liberal to the Party of the Right. The Union brings top national leaders to debate and interact with students on campus, including every US president since Eisenhower. Cultural centers also enrich college life and reach out into the New Haven community. Current cultural centers include Afro-American, Asian American, Puerto Rican, Chicano, and Native American; and the Joseph Slifka Center for Jewish Life at Yale.

Community Service – College students volunteer their services in a wide variety of public and community organizations, particularly in local schools. Through the Ulysses S. Grant Foundation for example, Yale students have helped many talented inner-city students improve and earn acceptance into colleges, and it also provides classroom-teaching experience for undergraduates. The graduate and professional schools also have active service organizations such as the Urban Resources Initiative, the Yale Urban Design Workshop, the Legal Services Organization, and HOPE (Homeless Outreach Program Enrichment).

Legacy

For three centuries, Yale alumni have made great societal contributions in a wide variety of fields. Most significantly, Yale graduates founded and led new colleges in the West and South and were chosen as first presidents of Princeton, Columbia, Dartmouth, Williams, Hamilton, Kenyon, Illinois, Wabash, Beloit, Cornell, Johns Hopkins, and the Universities of Georgia, Missouri, Mississippi, Wisconsin, Chicago, and California. Following is a selection of outstanding alumni and faculty grouped by subject. *Numbers in parentheses indicate Yale College class affiliation or other Yale school as noted.*

United States presidents

William Howard Taft (1878)
Gerald Ford (1941 law)
George Bush (1948)
William J. Clinton (1973 law)

Religious leaders

Jonathan Edwards (1720)	*Theologian and metaphysician*
Samuel Seabury (1748)	*First bishop of the American Episcopal Church*
Leonard Bacon (1820)	*Minister and antislavery leader whose writings influenced Abraham Lincoln*

Inventors

David Bushnell (1775)	*Submarine*
Eli Whitney (1792)	*Cotton gin and interchangeable parts*
Samuel F.B. Morse (1810)	*Telegraph*
Lee De Forest (1896, 1899 Ph.D.)	*Radio*
A.C. Gilbert (1909 medicine)	*Erector set, scientific toys*

Scientists

Benjamin Silliman (1796)	*Chemist*
Josiah Willard Gibbs (1858)	*Physicist*
Othniel Charles Marsh (1860)	*Paleontologist*
Maxine Singer (1957 Ph.D.)	*Biochemist*

Authors, journalists and playwrights

Joel Barlow (1778)
James Fenimore Cooper (1806)
Sinclair Lewis (1907)
Henry R. Luce (1920)
Thornton Wilder (1920)
William F. Buckley (1950)
A.R. Gurney (1958 drama)
John Guare (1963 drama)
Wendy Wasserstein (1976 drama)
John Hersey (1936)

Artists and architects

James Gamble Rogers (1889)
Frederic Remington (1900 art)
Mark Rothko (1925)
Eero Saarinen (1934 architecture)
Louis I. Kahn (1947-57 architecture faculty)
Claes Oldenburg (1950)
Paul Rand (1956-96 graphic design faculty)
Cesar Pelli (1977-84 dean, architecture)
Maya Lin (1981, 1986 architecture)

Composers

Charles Ives (1898)
Cole Porter (1913)
Douglas Moore (1915)
Roger Sessions (1933 music)
Mitch Leigh (1951 music)

Government Service

John C. Calhoun (1804)
Judah P. Benjamin (1828)
Samuel Tilden (1837)
Henry L. Stimson (1888)
W. Averell Harriman (1913)

Composers

Maury Yeston (1967, 1974 Ph.D.)

Paul Hindemith (1940-53 faculty)

Actors and directors

Monty Woolley (1911)

Elia Kazan (1933 drama)

Vincent Price (1933)

Julie Harris (1947 drama)

Paul Newman (1954 drama)

Sam Waterston (1962)

Henry Winkler (1970 drama)

Sigourney Weaver (1974 drama)

Meryl Streep (1975 drama)

David Hyde Pierce (1981)

Frances McDormand (1982 drama)

John Turturro (1983 drama)

Jodie Foster (1985)

Government Service

Dean Acheson (1916)

Stuart Symington (1923)

Chester Bowles (1924)

Cyrus Vance (1939, 1942 law)

George Pataki (1967)

George W. Bush (1968)

Strobe Talbott (1968)

Physicians

Harvey Cushing (1891)

Arnold Gesell (1915 medicine)

Benjamin Spock (1924)

Social scientists

William Graham Sumner (1863)

Irving Fisher (1888)

Athletes

Football

Twenty-six Yale men have been inducted into the College Football Hall of Fame including coaches **Walter Camp** and **Amos Alonzo Stagg** (1888), and 1936 and 1937 Heisman trophy winners **Larry Kelley** (1937) and **Clint Frank** (1938).

Other football stars include

President Gerald Ford (1941 law)
Junior Varsity coach, 1936-40

Levi Jackson (1950)

Brian Dowling (1969)

Calvin Hill (1969)

Richard Jauron (1973)

Stone Phillips (1977)

Baseball

President George Bush (1948, captain)

Ken MacKenzie (1956)

Ron Darling (1982)

Basketball

The very first game of college basketball with five men on each side was played in New Haven in March 1897, when Yale defeated Penn 32-10. Yale greats include **Tony Lavelli** (1949) and **Chris Dudley** (1987).

Swimming

Allen Stack (1949) — *1948 Olympic gold medallist and inventor of modern backstroke*

Don Schollander (1968) — *First swimmer in history to win 4 gold medals at one Olympics, 1964. World Athlete of the Year, 1964*

Boxing

Eddie Eagan (1921) — *1920 Olympic gold medallist and amateur heavyweight champion of both the US and England*

Track

Frank Shorter (1969) — *First American in 64 years to win the Olympic marathon, earning the gold medal in 1972*

Other notable alumni

Nathan Hale (1773)	*Revolutionary hero*
Noah Webster (1778)	*Creator of first American dictionary*
Edward Bouchet (1874, 1876)	*The first African American to graduate from Yale College and the first African American awarded the Ph.D. degree in the United States.*
Walter Camp (1880)	*Father of American football*
Gifford Pinchot (1889)	*Pioneer in conservation movement and founder of the US Forestry Service and the Yale School of Forestry*
Hiram A. Bingham (1896)	*Discoverer of Machu Picchu*
Robert Moses (1911)	*City planner*
John Hay Whitney (1924)	*Philanthropist and diplomat*
Paul Mellon (1929)	*Philanthropist*
Grace Hopper (1934 Ph.D.)	*Early computer scientist and developer of computer language COBOL, and the first woman to serve as US Naval Reserve Rear Admiral*
Garry Trudeau (1970, 1973 art)	*Creator of Doonesbury*
Hillary Rodham Clinton (1973 law)	*First Lady*

Nobel Prize Laureates

Physiology or Medicine

1934, George H. Whipple (1900)
1954, John F. Enders (1919)
1956, Dickinson Richards (1917)
1958, Joshua Lederberg (1948 Ph.D.)
1994, Alfred G. Gilman (1962)
1995, Eric Wieschaus (1974 Ph.D.)

Physics

1939, Ernest O. Lawrence (1925 Ph.D.)
1969, Murray Gell-Mann (1948)
1996, David Lee (1959 Ph.D.)

Chemistry

1968, Lars Onsager (1935 Ph.D.)
Yale professor

Literature

1930, Sinclair Lewis (1907)

Economics

1996, William Vickrey (1935)

Faculty awardees who were not Yale graduates include

Physiology or Medicine

1951, Max Theiler	Epidemiology Professor (1964-67)
1958, Edward L. Tatum	Biology Professor (1945-48)
1974, George E. Palade	Biology Professor (1973-present)

Economics

1975, Tjalling Koopmans	Economics Professor (1955-85)
1981, James Tobin	Economics Professor (1950-present)
1983, Gerard Debreu	Economics Professor (1955-62)

Physics

1955, Willis E. Lamb, Jr.	Physics Professor (1962-74)

Biology

1989, Sidney Altman	Biology Professor (1980-present)

For Further Reading

New Haven: A Guide to Architecture and Urban Design by Elizabeth Mills Brown (Yale University Press, New Haven, 1976)

New Haven: An Illustrated History edited by Floyd Shumway and Richard Hegel (Windsor Publications, 1987)

Yale: A History by Brooks Mather Kelley (Yale University Press, New Haven, 1974)

Yale: A Short History by George W. Pierson (Yale University, New Haven, 1979)

Yale University: An Architectural Tour by Patrick L. Pinnell (Princeton Architectural Press, New York, 1999)

Michael Marsland /Yale University

Engravings for Webster's dictionary from Sterling Memorial Library's Arts of the Book Collection

Three Centuries of Growth

The 1637 voyage of the Rev. **John Davenport** and **Theophilus Eaton** to America to fulfill Davenport's mission of establishing an "independent kingdom of Christ" and a college to educate its leaders resulted in the Puritans' settling in New Haven in 1638 and forming an independent colony. After years of instability however, the New Haven Colony was forced to unite with Connecticut in 1665, and the plan to establish a college could not be executed. In 1701, the Rev. **James Pierpont**'s distress at the declining state of the church resulted in his organizing a group of Connecticut ministers to meet and plan for the establishment of a college that would provide the colony with an educated clergy and civic leaders.

According to the first history of Yale published in 1766, "Each minister brought a Number of Books ...and laying them on the Table, said these words, or to this Effect: 'I give these books for founding a College in this Colony.'" In the same year New Haven was designated a co-capital of the colony with Hartford, and when the governor and General Assembly met in New Haven for the first time in October they passed "An Act for Liberty to Erect a Collegiate School." Its mission was to instruct youth in the arts and sciences and fit them "for Publick employment both in Church & Civil State." The new trustees then selected Saybrook at the mouth of the Connecticut River as the most convenient site for the school and **Abraham Pierson** a minister in Killingworth as the first Rector, or president. As Pierson's congregation would not release him from his contract, the college was headquartered in his home until his death in 1707.

After its brief residency in the unpopular Saybrook, in 1716 the Trustees voted to move the Collegiate School to New Haven, whose leaders promised to support it financially to a greater degree than Saybrook or Hartford. The famous donation of goods sold for £500 and books by **Elihu Yale**, as well as financial support from other residents, allowed for the completion of the first college building facing the Green, and in 1718 the school was renamed Yale College. With state appropriations, **Connecticut Hall**, the oldest standing Yale and New Haven building, was constructed in the early 1750s.

By the 1770s, students and alumni so actively supported the revolutionary cause that the British looked upon Yale as a hotbed of sedition. Yale patriots included Nathan Hale, Noah Webster, Joel Barlow, and Timothy Dwight. On July 3, 1779, it was Yale President **Ezra Stiles** who first spied the British forces in the New Haven harbor through his telescope in the steeple of the college chapel. The student militia helped defend the town on the next day.

Nate Leigh

Yale's president **Timothy Dwight** the elder, advanced the sciences in America by appointing **Benjamin Silliman** the first science professor in America in 1802. Over the next 50 years, Silliman developed both the arts and sciences by forming the first graduate school and a separate scientific school at Yale. Silliman worked to establish a medical school in 1810. He arranged for Yale to house John Trumbull's paintings in 1832, establishing the first university art gallery in the Western Hemisphere. Yale led the way in developing graduate and specialized school education in the arts and sciences as well, by establishing the Department of Philosophy and the Arts in 1846. In that year the first professorships in agriculture and applied chemistry were created, and in 1852 the engineering school and the degree of bachelor of philosophy (science) were created. This instruction was consolidated in 1854 into the Yale Scientific School. Renamed the Sheffield Scientific School, it became Connecticut's first land-grant college. Another focus of the department led to Yale's awarding of the first doctor of philosophy degrees in America in 1861. In 1876 New Haven native **Edward Bouchet** received the degree of Doctor of Philosophy from Yale, the first doctorate awarded to an African American by an American university.

In the 1820s the divinity and law schools were established, and by mid-century Yale was the largest college in the US. In 1869 the first university art school was opened with the donation of a New Haven alumnus, Augustus Street, and his wife, Caroline, who specified that the school be coed. In the 1870s, the Peabody Museum opened to showcase the dinosaur and other bones and fossils collected by Professor **O.C. Marsh** and his "bonediggers" on Western expeditions. By 1880 Yale enrollment had reached 1,000, and in 1887 Yale College changed its name to Yale University. Women were admitted to the graduate school in 1892; in 1894 seven received doctor of philosophy degrees. From 1870 to 1899, the faculty grew from 65 to 260, and the student body from 755 to 2,684. Another new professional school, the forestry school, was established at the turn of the century by Yale College alumnus **Gifford Pinchot.** College sports and its associated traditions were largely developed at Yale, beginning with the first rowing races in the New Haven harbor in 1843. Perhaps Yale's greatest sports contributions have been in the field of football, owing mainly to **Walter Camp,** Class of 1880, who transformed the rough and tumble game of rugby into American football. Yale's football glory years extended from that time through the 1930s, when two of the first three Heisman trophy winners were Yale men. Its greatest football heroes were in fact fictional, Dink Stover, main character of the best selling novel, *Stover at Yale,* and Frank Merriwell whose exploits were followed in 250 dime novels. The **Yale Bowl** the largest stadium constructed since the Roman Colosseum upon its completion in 1914, was filled with a record 80,000 fans for the Yale-Harvard game of 1920.

Yale's great teachers and researchers earned international reputations in the late 19C and early 20C, such as physicist **Josiah Willard Gibbs**; **William Dwight Whitney**, linguist and lexicographer; **William Graham Sumner**, the first sociologist; and William Lyon Phelps, the first teacher of modern literature. In contrast, the college students seemed more content to earn a gentleman's C, and devote their attention to athletics, fraternities and senior societies. Their social life became more private when the **Yale Fence** on which generations of students had sat facing the city was finally removed in 1888. New construction of large stone dormitories hid The Old Brick Row and physically separated the university from the city. New schools and halls such as the Divinity School, the Berkeley Oval, and the Old Peabody Museum were built and later replaced.

For two centuries all of Yale's presidents had been ministers, but in 1899 the Corporation elected a lay president for the first time, **Arthur Twining Hadley**, an economist specializing in railroad legislation. In the first quarter of the century Yale made further advances in the education of women, awarding the first honorary degree to a woman, **Jane Addams** in 1910; admitting women to the medical school in 1916 and to the law school in 1919; and establishing a school of nursing in 1923. During this time Yale and New Haven continued to grow apart physically and socially. The need for change became evident after the end of World War I. Town-gown relations sank to a low point in May 1919 when veteran versus student protests led to rioting.

The completion of campus and city icon Harkness Tower symbolized a new stage in university development. President **James Rowland Angell**'s administration (1921-37) benefited from a large bequest by **John William Sterling** and donations from the Harkness family which allowed for educational reform through the implementation and construction of the residential colleges as well as a broadening and growth of the graduate and professional schools and libraries. Sterling's grandest memorial is the Sterling Memorial Library completed in 1930. Featuring the largest library stack tower constructed to that time, Sterling has become the hub of a library system that is one of the world's largest. **Edward S. Harkness**, Class of 1897, transformed Yale, first in the area of the arts by gifts to establish a drama school in 1924 and construct a new art gallery completed in 1928. In 1930, Yale accepted his plan and funds to construct and endow the undergraduate residential college system to develop closer student-teacher relationships and provide manageable social units composed of cross-sections of the student body. As tuition remained low, less affluent New Haveners took advantage of their close proximity to the ivory tower as a step toward upward mobility. Yale's expansive building programs which resulted in the razing of many buildings continued even through the Great Depression prompting the humorous toast, "Here's to Good Old Yale, Tear Her Down, Tear Her Down."

The transformation of the campus into a military training base during World War II put Yale in the spotlight as it prepared over 20,000 men and women for war service and was home to Glenn Miller's air force band and his weekly broadcasts from Woolsey Hall. In the 1950s and early 60s, President **A. Whitney Griswold** lay the foundation for contemporary Yale both educationally and architecturally by redefining its liberal arts educational mission and commissioning building designs by the best modern architects. Under the administration of President **Kingman Brewster**, Yale became more democratic and diverse. Women were admitted to Yale College in 1969, and the first women transfer students received the bachelor of arts degree in 1971. After the civil strife of the late 1960s and early 70s, the university and the community forged new methods of collaboration in developing the downtown site for the Yale Center for British Art. Through the administrations of Yale presidents **A. Bartlett Giamatti**, **Benno Schmidt**, and current president **Richard C. Levin**, Yale and the city have continued to work cooperatively on educational, cultural, and economic projects.

LAWS of Yale College, 1787

I. If any Scholar shall be guilty of Blasphemy, Cursing, Robbery, Fornication, Forgery, or any such attrocious Crime, he shall be immediately expelled.

II. If any Scholar shall deny the holy Scriptures, or any part thereof, to be of divine Authority, or shall assert any Error or Heresy, subverting the Foundation of the Christian Religion, and shall continue obstinate therein, after the first and second Admonition, he shall be expelled.

III. If any Scholar shall be guilty of a profane Oath or Vow, of profaning the Name, Word, or Ordinances of God; of contemptuous refractory Carriage towards his Superiors; of Fighting, Striking, Quarrelling, Challenging turbulent Words or Behaviour, Drunkenness, Lasciviousness, wearing Womens' Apparel, Fraud, Injustice, Idleness, Lying, Defamation, or any such like Crime, he shall be punished by Fine, Admonition, Rustication, or even Expulsion, as the Nature and Circumstances of the Crime may require.

Evolution of the Campus

The Collegiate School was housed in a variety of private residences in Saybrook and other Connecticut communities from 1701 until its establishment in New Haven in 1716. After receiving Elihu Yale's donation, the first permanent building erected in New Haven in 1717-18 was named Yale College. A relief sculpture mounted on the exterior wall of **Bingham Hall**, which presently occupies the site at the corner of College and Chapel Streets, commemorates the long, narrow wooden building that served as dormitory, chapel, classroom, library, and dining hall. Other reliefs recall the beginnings of Yale College and **The Fence.** Yale gradually acquired the land in the rest of the block bounded by High and Elm Streets that is known today as the Old Campus. In 1750-53, Connecticut Hall was constructed and still stands as the oldest building on the campus and in New Haven. On its south side, the First Chapel was constructed in 1761-63. In 1792, James Hillhouse, the father of New Haven city planning, asked **John Trumbull**, the noted artist of the American Revolution, to draw up a plan for the future development of the college. The **Trumbull Plan** consisted of a single row of Georgian and Federal brick dormitories alternating with towered religious and academic halls facing the New Haven Green. Later called the **Old Brick Row** it was the first planned college campus in America. The Georgian style used for many types of buildings in the 18C and early 19C, especially for factories, became unfashionable by the 1840s, and Yale selected the Victorian Gothic style of design for most of its new constructions.

Manuscripts and Archives /Yale University

The Fence

The first Gothic building on the Old Campus was the Library, now **Dwight Hall**, erected behind the Old Brick Row in the early 1840s. The Art Building, later renamed **Street Hall**, after donors Augustus and Caroline Street, was constructed during the Civil War. After the war, Yale undertook a new building program to enclose the Old Brick Row within a perimeter of substantial Victorian Gothic dormitories and academic halls. Wealthy donors, both alumni and others, provided ample funds over the next quarter of a century to construct imposing halls designed by the most fashionable New York architects, including **Russell Sturgis, Jr.**, **J. Cleveland Cady**, **Charles Haight** and **Bruce Price**. After the completion of the newer buildings, the old buildings in the center of the campus were demolished, leaving a large open courtyard for student activities. By the time of the celebration of Yale's Bicentennial in 1901, all of the Old Brick Row had been demolished with the exception of Connecticut Hall.

Beyond the Old Campus

As Yale developed new courses of undergraduate instruction and graduate and professional schools in the 19C, it began to expand beyond the Old Campus. Beginning in 1859, along a small street facing the Old Library, appropriately named Library Street, Yale built for the undergraduates a gymnasium and science buildings that were later torn down when the Memorial Quadrangle was constructed. To the far north, at the corner of Grove and Prospect Streets, the Sheffield Scientific School campus was constructed starting in 1860. Its main building incorporated the first home of the Yale

Michael Marsland /Yale University

Medical School dating from 1813. Across Elm Street, in the area now occupied by Berkeley and Calhoun Colleges and the Cross Campus, Yale built an elegant Divinity School (1869-81) in High Victorian Gothic style, and a campus for freshmen called the Berkeley Oval, in Renaissance Revival style.
To commemorate the 200th anniversary of its founding in 1901, Yale received funds to construct the Bicentennial Buildings and Woodbridge Hall around the new University Quadrangle. Later named the Hewitt University Quadrangle, it is now commonly called **Beinecke Plaza**. The Bicentennial Buildings in classic Beaux Arts style consist of a monumental dining hall, a grand auditorium, and Memorial Hall in remembrance of Yale men killed in the Civil War and other American wars. Woodbridge Hall is the central administration building. A large World War I memorial colonnade and cenotaph was added in 1927. The quadrangle, completed in the 1960s with the construction of the Beinecke Rare Book and Manuscript Library, physically links the liberal arts and scientific campuses of the university.

The New Yale

The harmonious groupings of Collegiate Gothic buildings in the central campus that symbolize "Old Yale" were actually constructed in the years between the First and Second World Wars. Evoking, but not replicating the architectural styles of the colleges of Oxford and Cambridge, the Memorial Quadrangle (1917-21) marked the new era in building construction for the university. The gift of Mrs. Stephen V. Harkness in memory of her son, Charles W. Harkness, Class of 1883, the quadrangle across High Street from the Old Campus was comprised of **Harkness Tower**, the major Yale landmark, and two dormitory quadrangles that were later converted into Branford and Saybrook Colleges. **James Gamble Rogers** was then appointed architect for the General Plan for the university. In 1918, **John William Sterling**, Class of 1864, left a bequest to Yale of over $15,000,000 that grew to nearly $40,000,000. His bequest funded the construction of the Sterling Memorial Library, Sterling Law Buildings, Sterling Hall of Medicine, Sterling Divinity Quadrangle, Sterling Power Plant, Sterling Chemical Laboratory, and the Hall of Graduate Studies. In the 1920s, **Edward S. Harkness**, Class of 1897, the brother of Charles, contributed to the construction of the Drama School and the Art Gallery. To promote closer student-teacher relationships and improve the social life of the undergraduates, he donated funds to establish at Yale a residential college system based on the systems in Oxford and Cambridge. In 1933, the first group of residential colleges was opened—Branford, Calhoun, Davenport, Jonathan Edwards, Pierson, Saybrook, and Trumbull, followed by Berkeley, Timothy Dwight, and Silliman. While the style of the majority of the colleges is Gothic, four are Georgian Revival: Timothy Dwight, Pierson, Davenport (except for the Gothic York Street side), and Silliman (apart from the older incorporated buildings). The street sides of the colleges are enhanced by low-walled moats filled with greenery and flowering plants and trees. Planned by Beatrix Farrand, the noted landscape architect and designer of Yale's courtyards and gardens, they are especially beautiful in the spring.

Yale and Modern Architecture

President A. Whitney Griswold (1950-63), a great supporter of the arts, introduced a new Yale architectural policy. Instead of continuing the unified Collegiate Gothic style of James Gamble Rogers, he chose to invite the best modern architects to submit plans for Yale buildings. The first commission was the 1953 addition to the 1928 Art Gallery designed by **Louis Kahn**, then a professor of architecture at Yale University. It was his first major work. Notably, his last work, completed in 1977 after his death, was the Yale Center for British Art. In 1957, construction began on the David S. Ingalls Skating Rink by **Eero Saarinen**. Saarinen was innovative as an architect in advocating the guiding principle that form should follow function. For that reason, his constructions do not have a "trademark" style. In addition to the Jefferson Memorial Arch in St. Louis, Saarinen designed Dulles International Airport near Washington, DC and the TWA Terminal at the John Fitzgerald Kennedy (JFK) Airport in New York. Both are notable for their flight-inspired wing-like shapes. At Yale, Saarinen also designed the Morse and Stiles Residential Colleges (1960-62) that combine modern and medieval Italian elements. The Beinecke Rare Book and Manuscript Library by **Gordon Bunshaft**, of the firm Skidmore, Owings & Merrill was completed in 1963. Bunshaft's Lever House in New York City had influenced American architecture. He later designed the Lyndon Baines Johnson Presidential Library in Austin, TX and the Hirshhorn Museum and Sculpture Garden in Washington, DC. The same year marked the completion of the Art and Architecture Building designed by **Paul Rudolph** when he was chairman of the architecture department. The nine-story building features 36 level changes. Best known for his megastructures in East and Southeast Asia, Rudolph also designed the Temple Street Parking Garage in New Haven. From 1963-65, **Philip Johnson Associates** constructed the Laboratory of Epidemiology and Public Health and the Kline Science Center, including the Kline Geology Laboratory, Kline Chemistry Laboratory, and the Kline Biology Tower. Johnson is best known as co-architect of the Seagram Building and the New York State Theater, Lincoln Center, New York City. He is also known for his glass house in New Canaan, Connecticut.

The Yale Athletic Grounds

The **Yale Bowl** *(see p 51)*, at Derby Avenue on the New Haven-West Haven border, is the principal facility in the Yale athletic complex. The formal entrance to the grounds is the **Walter Camp Field Gateway**, a national memorial erected in 1927-28, from contributions received from over 500 schools and colleges and Yale alumni in honor of **Walter Camp**, Class of 1880, the father of American football. Across the street is Yale Field, home of the Yale baseball team and the New Haven Ravens professional baseball team. Other athletic facilities in the complex include the **Connecticut Tennis Center**, featuring over 30 tennis courts and the third largest tennis stadium in the world; **Coxe Cage**, the home of the Yale men's and women's indoor track and field teams; and the Yale Soccer-Lacrosse Stadium.
A committee of Yale alumni designed and raised funds to construct the Yale Bowl as a replacement for the old Yale Field, home of the football team since 1884. The Yale football team was one of the most popular teams in America in a time when collegiate football drew more fans than professional teams.

Manuscripts and Archives / Yale University

The CAMPUS★★★

Time: 2 days
Map of Principal Sights p 6
Yale Visitor Information Center ☎ 203-432-2300 or www.yale.edu/visitor

Not only a campus of beautiful buildings and a citizenry energized by higher learning, but the inspiration of some of our nation's most prized pastimes and heralded heroes and heroines. Explore its pathways, and experience the dynamism of this spectacular university setting.

WALKING TOURS

The campus tours are divided into two itineraries, Central Campus, and Hillhouse Avenue and Science Hill. Make your first stop for either tour the Yale Visitor Information Center where you can obtain brochures about the university. It is recommended that visitors park at one of the many downtown garages. Public restrooms are available only at the Visitor Information Center, museums, and libraries.

Yale Visitor Information Center – *149 Elm St. Open year-round Mon–Fri 9am–4:45pm, weekends 10am–4pm. ☎ 203-432-2300 www.yale.edu/visitor.* Historically known as the Pierpont House, this simple two-story Georgian Colonial white frame structure is the oldest surviving house in New Haven. The Rev. James Pierpont, principal founder of Yale University and minister of what is now Center Church, constructed an earlier house on the site in the late 1600s. The current structure, a center-hall, center-chimney design, dates to 1767 and is situated on Elm Street's "Quality Row," in the lot originally designated as the site for a college by New Haven's founders. Its first occupant was John Pierpont, grandson of James Pierpont. During the brief British occupation of New Haven, the invaders used the Pierpont home for their headquarters and hospital. Bloodstains on the central staircase have consequently inspired legends that the house was haunted. Members of the Pierpont family occupied the house until 1900 when Anson Phelps Stokes, secretary of Yale University, bought it for his private residence. Upon Stokes' resignation in 1921, the house was purchased by Yale University and converted into the Yale Faculty Club. The building served as the Yale Admissions Office from 1977 to 1995, when it became the Yale Visitor Information Center.

Central Campus *Map p 40*

Turn right out of the Visitor Information Center. Proceed up Elm St. and cross College St. Turn left at College St. crossing Elm St. and continue to Phelps Hall and Archway.

Phelps Hall and Archway – The Archway through Phelps Hall is the symbolic entrance to Yale University. Completed in 1896, **Phelps Hall** (Charles Coolidge Haight) was the final link connecting **Welch Hall** (Bruce Price, 1891) to its left and **Lawrance Hall** (Russell Sturgis Jr, 1885-86) on the right in the new High Victorian Gothic quadrangle begun on the **Old Campus★** after the Civil War. Modeled on a Tudor gatehouse, the imposing tower is surmounted with four turrets and pierced by an oval archway that frames a view of the Old Library, **Dwight Hall** (Henry Austin, 1842-46) across the campus. When Dink Stover, the immortal fictional hero, passed through its portals for the first time and felt its "great protecting embrace," he said "reverently ... and this is it—this is Yale." Today most of the Old Campus buildings serve as freshmen dormitories and administrative offices.

Proceed through Phelps Archway and walk left to Connecticut Hall.

★**Connecticut Hall** – Built in 1750 and constructed of brick in a simple Georgian Colonial style by masons Francis Letort and Thomas Bills, this hall remains the oldest standing Yale and New Haven building. Named in honor of the Connecticut Assembly, the hall originally had eight studies or parlors with two attached bedrooms for students to share. In addition to rent, students were charged a penny a week to cover the expense of sweeping the floors and making beds. John Trumbull remodeled the hall in 1797 from three to four stories as part of his design for the Old Brick Row *(p 34)*. In 1885 the first Yale Co-op Bookstore *(p 72)* opened in the building and remained there for 20 years. Serving mainly as a dormitory, it was also used for meetings and instruction. From 1909-1941, it held the offices of the Dean of Yale College. Today it provides a reading room for Freshmen, the Yale College faculty meeting room, seminar rooms, and two guest suites. When the rest of the Old Brick Row was demolished in 1900, Connecticut Hall was saved as a memorial to Yale's past and restored to its original three stories. In 1965 it was designated a National Historic Landmark. Its last restoration and remodeling took place in 1952-54, under the direction of architects Douglas Orr and Richard A. Kimball.

Michael Marsland /Yale University

Connecticut Hall

Crafted in bronze by Bela Lyon Pratt in 1898, this portrayal of **Nathan Hale [1]** in a powerful and patriotic stance pays homage to America's first spy, who roomed in Connecticut Hall. After graduating in 1773 at the age of 18, he taught school and then enlisted in the fight for independence. Hale volunteered to carry out an intelligence mission for General Washington. When captured by the British in New York, he was carrying his Yale diploma to support his cover identity as a schoolteacher. Hale's immortal words uttered before his execution in 1776 appear around the base: "I only regret that I have but one life to lose for my country."

Return past Phelps Archway and Lawrance and Farnam Halls.

Battell Chapel – The university's spiritual center and the largest house of worship on campus was completed in 1876 as a Civil War Memorial. Architect of both **Farnam** and **Durfee Halls**, Russell Sturgis, Jr. designed the High Victorian Gothic chapel to fill the gap between these two buildings. Carved capitals and a seemingly woven stone exterior form a prelude to the elaborate interior. In the vestibule, on the site of the Old Divinity School, a small display highlights Yale's role in the Amistad Affair *(p 70)*. It also marks a site on the Connecticut Freedom Trail, locations associated with the heritage and movement towards freedom of African Americans during slavery. Sunday worship *(11am)* is held here in the Protestant tradition. The chapel is also home to the Church of Christ at Yale.

Walk across campus toward Harkness Memorial Tower.

Dwight Hall – Constructed in 1842 and designed by Henry Austin, the former Old Library and Yale's first Gothic Revival building established the style used in the Old Campus quadrangle built around the Old Brick Row. Copper-domed Tudor towers adorn the Portland brownstone structure. The hall now contains Dwight Memorial Chapel, the student social action center at Yale, and meeting rooms.

Immediately in front of Dwight Hall sits the statue of **Theodore Dwight Woolsey [2]**, honoring Yale's mid-19C president (1846-71). Sculpted by John Ferguson Weir, the bronze representation portrays a pensive Woolsey gazing through Phelps archway—his shoe shiny from Yale students rubbing his toe for good luck.

The **Abraham Pierson statue [3]** is also known as the "Hank statue" because of the Latin inscription *Hanc Statuam*... on the back side of its base. This 1874 bronze sculpture by Launt Thompson pays homage to Yale's first president, or rector. A minister in Killingworth, Connecticut, Pierson was elected rector of the Collegiate School in 1701. His parishioners would not release him from his contract, however, so he opened the college in his home, where it continued until his

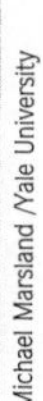
Michael Marsland /Yale University

death in 1707. The **Giamatti Bench [4]**, carved out of two granite blocks, honors A. Bartlett Giamatti, Yale president (1978-86) and Commissioner of Baseball (1989). Giamatti said that from this vantage point the Old Campus looked like a baseball diamond. Inscribed on the bench is the quotation: "A liberal education is at the heart of a civilized society, and at the heart of a liberal education is teaching."

Continue past the Giamatti Bench to High St.

★**Harkness Memorial Tower** – *Fronting Branford College on High St.* The major landmark and icon of the university, this 216ft Gothic tower designed by James Gamble Rogers was completed in 1921 as part of the Memorial Quadrangle, now Branford and Saybrook Colleges. Observe the carving over the Memorial Gateway across the street, bearing the Yale motto, "For God, for Country, and for Yale." The tower is embellished with dozens of sculptures celebrating Yale's history, traditions, and notable alumni. The most visible images are figures in the niches on

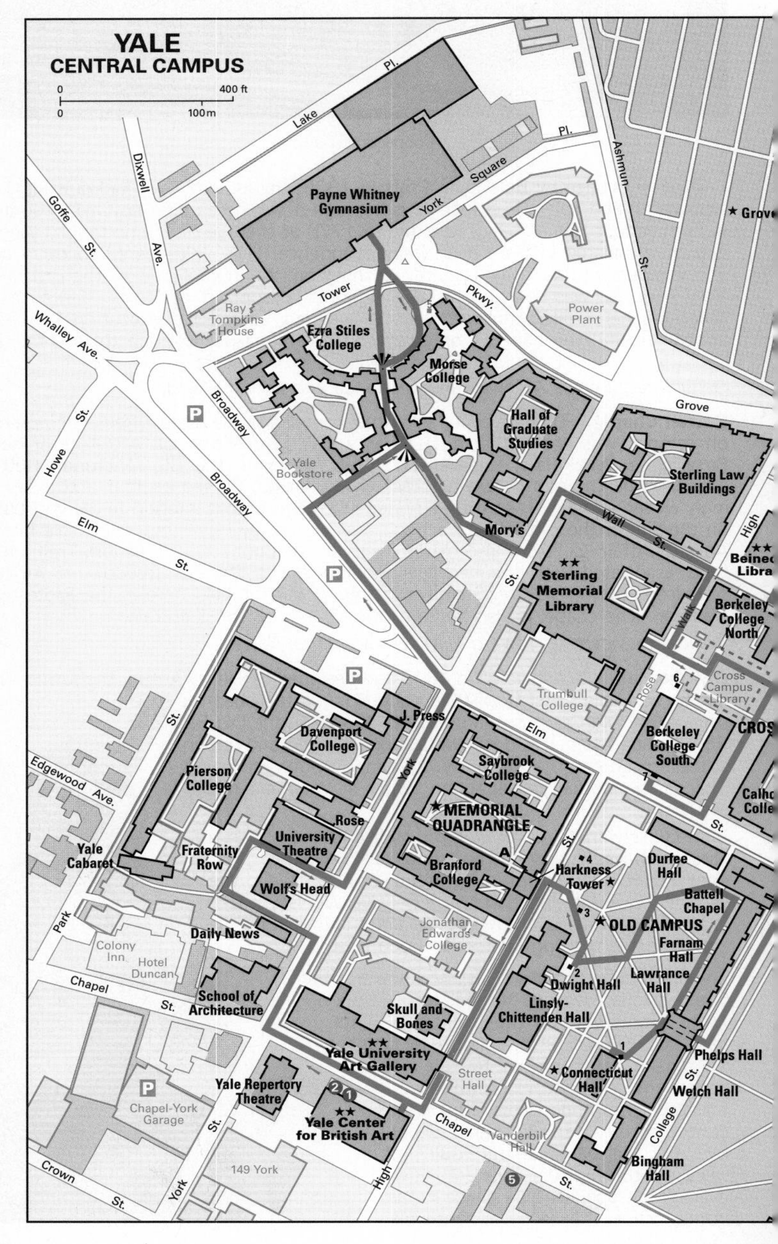

either side of the clock faces. Proceeding clockwise from High Street are Elihu Yale, Jonathan Edwards, Nathan Hale, Noah Webster, James Fenimore Cooper, John C. Calhoun, Samuel F.B. Morse, and Eli Whitney. Farther up are representations of professions, qualities of life, Yale students as soldiers in American wars, and caricatures of students as gargoyles. The tower houses a 44-bell carillon that is frequently played by student and professional carilloneurs.

The **Memorial Gate [A]** beside Harkness Tower was crafted by the master metalsmith Samuel Yellin (1885-1940).

Turn left and continue down High St. To the left sits Linsly-Chittenden Hall and across High St. is Skull and Bones.

Linsly-Chittenden Hall – These former turn-of-the-century libraries have recently been renovated into state-of-the art electronic classrooms and faculty offices, and restored to their original Art Nouveau beauty. "Linsly-Chitt" originally began as two separate structures with round-arched Chittenden (J. Cleveland Cady, 1888) as an

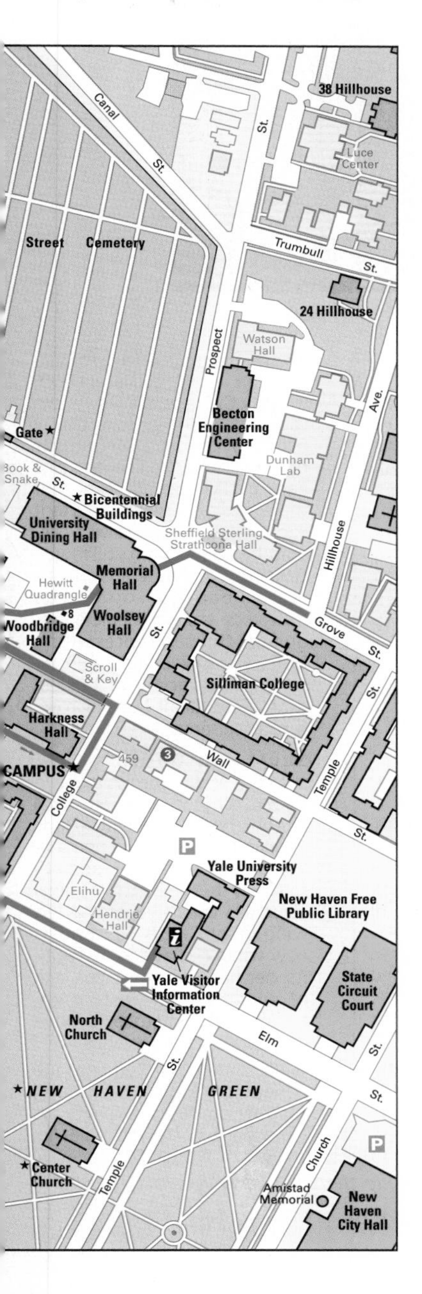

Michael Marsland /Yale University

Tiffany Window, Linsly-Chittenden Hall

Secret Societies

The most mysterious buildings on campus are the houses, or "tombs," of the Yale senior societies commonly known as "secret societies." Each society has 15 members, seniors selected in April of their junior year by the outgoing seniors. The oldest, Skull and Bones, founded in 1832, includes among its alumni, President George Bush and his father Senator Prescott Bush, and journalists William F. Buckley, and Henry Luce. Scattered about the campus, in architectural styles varying from classic Greek temples to an 18C townhouse, the "tombs" share a common element—the absence of windows. The rituals performed behind the sealed facades are not divulged to non-members, but reported activities include twice-weekly meetings, elaborate dinners, and the presentation of autobiographies or confessions. These former bastions of male bonding are all now coed and diverse in their membership. Look for the unique structures that are home to Berzelius, Book and Snake, Elihu, Manuscript, St. Elmo's, Scroll and Key, Skull and Bones, and Wolf's Head.

annex to the Old Library (Dwight Hall). Linsly, (1906, Charles C. Haight) with its octagonal towers, eventually bridged the two structures both physically and stylistically. Facing High Street is one of the largest and most important early **stained glass windows★** created by Louis Comfort Tiffany. Gracing Chittenden Library's main reading room, the 30ft-wide triptych depicts allegorical figures representing forms of knowledge and inspiration in a variety of opalescent and brilliant hues of rose, turquoise, and gold.

Skull and Bones – Constructed of dark brownstone in 1856, this Greek Revival "tomb" boasting Egypto-Doric detailing serves as the home of Yale's oldest senior society founded in 1832. The original structure consisted of the left wing *(from High St.)* until a new wing was added in 1903. Its hermetic appearance, lack of windows and austere entrance are ubiquitous features of all the senior societies.

Walk under the Romanesque "bridge of thighs" connecting *(at left)* the first university art school building, Street Hall (Peter B. Wight, 1864) and *(right)*, the old Yale Art Gallery (1928), now the Department of the History of Art, to Chapel Street.

Cross High St. and continue on Chapel St. to the Yale University Art Gallery.

★★**Yale University Art Gallery** – *Description p 58.*

Cross Chapel St.

★★**Yale Center for British Art** – *Description p 54.*

Upon exiting the Yale Center for British Art, continue up Chapel St. to the Yale Repertory Theatre.

Yale Repertory Theatre – *1120 Chapel St. Performances Aug–May. ☎ 203-432-1234.* Established in 1966 in the former Calvary Baptist Church building, this professional theater links theoretical study with production work for experienced theatre artists. Productions are presented to the public throughout the academic year.

Cross Chapel St. Continue up York St.

School of Architecture – *Exhibits in the building are open to the public free of charge year-round Mon–Sat 9am–5pm. ☎ 203-432-2288.* The Art and Architecture Building (1963), popularly known as A & A, was designed by former chairman Paul Rudolph. While it has been at the center of architectural controversy since its construction, the building is a prime example of Rudolph's urban modernist style. The strong ribbed vertical lines of its corrugated surfaces were produced by pouring concrete into wooden forms. After stripping away the forms, the concrete edges were hammered to expose the aggregate. The nine-story structure is split into 36 levels defined more by floors and ceilings than walls. Above the street-level library, there is a two-story exhibition hall.

Proceed to 202 York St.

1 Atticus Bookstore-Cafe

1082 Chapel St. ☎ 203-776-4040. Coffee, pastries, breads, and sandwiches await you at this bookshop/cafe. Peruse the stacks or read your favorite newspaper while you wait for a latté.

2 Scoozzi

1104 Chapel St. ☎ 203-776-8268. ww.scoozzi.com. From the Yale Center for British Art, head up the street and down the stairs to this seemingly subterranean trattoria and wine bar whose *insalate*, pasta, and risotto offer the perfect nourishment for museum hopping.

Yale Daily News – "The oldest college daily" newspaper (since 1878) located at 202 York Street has trained many famous journalists including Henry Luce, of *Time* magazine fame, and William F. Buckley.

Take a detour around **Fraternity Row**. Along this posh alley, elegant slate-roofed fraternity houses were constructed around 1930 to replace the structures demolished in the rebuilding of the university. Today they house a variety of student organizations, including the **Yale Cabaret** *(217 Park St.; ☎ 203-432-1566)*, where drama students present plays and musical productions and offer light dining.

Return back through the gateway and take the small alley around **Wolf's Head** *(210 York St.)*, another senior society. Stop at the **University Theatre** *(222 York St.; performances Aug–May; ☎ 203-432-1212)* home of the drama school and the undergraduate association of long tradition, The Dramat. Notable drama school alumni include Paul Newman, Meryl Streep, and Henry Winkler.

Continue up York St.

Rose Alumni House – *232 York St.* Originally a fraternity house, this Gothic Revival cottage now provides offices and meeting rooms for the Association of Yale Alumni and serves as the on-campus center for returning alumni.

Continue on York St.

Pierson and Davenport Colleges – Designed by James Gamble Rogers, these residential colleges (1933) exemplify a discrete symbiosis of architectural style and use of space. While the bulk of Pierson parallels Park Street, its stone and iron gateway at No. 236 York Street contrasts the subdued entrance of Davenport at No. 248. Pierson's Georgian tower marks the entrance to its main courtyard that leads to the "Slave Quarters," offering a peek at its Charlestonian aesthetic. Davenport's Georgian façade is crowned by a tower modeled after the tower atop Boston's Old State House. Facing York Street, its Gothic Revival elements harmonize with the Memorial Quadrangle and surrounding colleges.

Across the street, comprising the **Memorial Quadrangle**★, lie **Branford** and **Saybrook Colleges** (James Gamble Rogers; 1921, 1933). Branford joins with Harkness Tower *(p 40)* while Saybrook is crowned by **Wrexham Tower**, modeled after that of St. Giles Church in Wrexham, Wales, where Elihu Yale is buried in the churchyard.

Continue up York Street and past **J. Press** men's clothier *(No. 262)*, one of the last of several fine tailoring shops that has served generations of Yale men.

Cross Elm St. and turn left onto Broadway. Proceed to the Yale Bookstore. Walk through the passageway of the bookstore to Ezra Stiles College. Turn left onto the steps separating the colleges and proceed toward the gymnasium.

Morse and Stiles Colleges – The last of the 12 undergraduate residential colleges were completed in 1962. Named for inventor and artist Samuel F. B. Morse (Class of 1810), and Ezra Stiles, Yale president (1778-95), they were designed by the noted architect Eero Saarinen ('34), who also designed the Ingalls Skating Rink *(p 48)*. Saarinen innovatively combines avant garde and traditional elements in his use of rubble-finished concrete to create the effect of an Italian hill town. The steps between the almost symmetrically placed buildings allow for **views** of Payne Whitney Gym to the north and of Harkness Tower to the south.

Cross Tower Parkway.

Payne Whitney Gymnasium – Nicknamed the "Cathedral of Sweat," the gymnasium is a memorial to Payne Whitney, Class of 1898. A gift by his family, including his son, sportsman and diplomat John Hay Whitney ('26), the massive Gothic building constructed of Briar Hill sandstone, when completed in 1932, reigned as the largest gymnasium in the world and with its new addition remains one of the grandest. Along with its sponsorship of 30 varsity sports and over 30 club sports, Yale supports a wide range of intramural and extracurricular programs from swimming and rowing to basketball, including those that present significant opportunities for recreational and instructional participation for all students, faculty, and staff. Enter the lobby and view the original and the dignified **Handsome Dan I** *(p 25)*, the first Yale bulldog mascot of the 1890s.

Return through Morse and Stiles Colleges. As you leave the gym, check out Claes Oldenburg's sculpture, Lipstick [5], in the Morse court. Continue along the pathway to the left to York St. Turn left at 306 York St., Mory's. Proceed up York St. to the Hall of Graduate Studies.

Hall of Graduate Studies – Completed in 1932, Yale's most modernistic interpretation of the Gothic style features a unique Art Deco metal tower reminiscent of New York's Chrysler Building. Its recently renovated **lounge★** features a dazzling gilded and painted ceiling, and stained-glass windows depicting often fantastic images of the sciences and technology in tones of acid yellow etched in black.

■ Mory's

306 York St. ☎ *203-562-3157.* A private eating club steeped in tradition, Mory's traces its roots back through the 19C to a public house near the New Haven harbor. A favorite refreshment stop for Yale rowers, it moved downtown where it was known as The Quiet House, then to Temple Street where it was named Mory's Temple Bar. In 1912, the Yale singing group the Whiffenpoofs rescued Mory's from bankruptcy by transforming it into a private Yale College club and moved it to this Federal frame house. Membership qualifications have been expanded to include women and a range of students, faculty, and professional staff. The interior is crowded with sports memorabilia and old carved oak tables. Home to the various Yale a cappella singing groups, Mory's celebrated Whiffs continue to entertain patrons on Monday nights, concluding with their trademark rendition of the "Whiffenpoof Song."

Nate leigh

Humorous details abound in the construction material and decoration, including bricks impressed with winged heads in deference to the Yale president James Rowland Angell (1920-37). The carved heads over the entrance depict not lofty deans and professors, but the construction engineers and supervisors who worked on the building. To this day who authorized these whimsical creations remains a mystery.

Cross York St. to Wall St.

Sterling Law Buildings – One of the many Yale schools and buildings funded by the great bequest of John William Sterling in 1918, this James Gamble Rogers creation was completed in 1932. Decorated with often humorous sculptural depictions of crime and punishment characteristic of Rogers' Modern Gothic style, the buildings provide all of the academic and living facilities required by its students.

Proceed to the corner of High and Wall Sts. Cross Wall St. to Rose Walk, between Sterling Library and Berkeley College.

★★Sterling Memorial Library – *Description p 49.*

Directly in front of Sterling Library's main entrance lies the **Women's Table [6]**. Celebrated for her work on the Vietnam War Memorial in Washington, DC, Yale College ('81) and School of Architecture graduate ('86) **Maya Lin** designed the table in honor of the 20th anniversary (1969) of coeducation in the college. Dedicated in 1993, its understated composition, a thin sheet of water flowing across a circular, polished granite table, records the number of women registered in all schools of the university since its founding in 1701. The first women students were formally registered in the art school in 1873.

Walk down the steps and through **Cross Campus★** (past the subterranean undergraduate Cross Campus Library) between the two halves of **Berkeley College** (James Gamble Rogers, 1933), named in honor of Anglo-Irish Anglican bishop, philosopher, and scientist George Berkeley, who endowed the first graduate study program at Yale in 1733. Don't miss the Our Lady of the Telephone **tablet [7]** located on the Elm Street side of the exterior about the middle of the building—a reminder of the site's use as Yale's first telephone exchange. Continuing through Cross Campus, to the right is **Calhoun College** (John Russell Pope, 1932), named for John C. Calhoun (1804), South Carolina statesman and US vice president, in a symbolic move toward reconciliation with the southern states after the Civil War. On the left lies **Harkness Hall** (William Adams Delano, 1927), a classroom building.

Naples Pizza & Restaurant

90 Wall St. ☎ 203-776-9021. For the quintessential higher education dining experience—i.e. lots of good food at low, low prices—break bread at Naples, complete with old wooden dining tables and booths and decorated with Yale memorabilia. All of campus comes together to partake of its big slices of pizza, burgers, and hearty daily specials.

Turn left at Harkness Hall on to College St. Continue up College St. and cross Wall St. Turn left up Wall St. past the senior society Scroll and Key (right) and proceed on to the Hewitt Quadrangle, known as Beinecke Plaza.

★★Beinecke Rare Book and Manuscript Library – *Open year-round Mon–Fri 8:30am–5pm, Sat 10am–5pm. Hours may vary during summer sessions and school breaks. www.library.yale.edu. ☎ 203-432-2977.* This floating box of translucent Vermont marble panes framed in granite is one of the largest buildings in the world devoted entirely to 600,000 rare books and manuscripts. A Gordon Bunshaft design completed in 1963, the building features an amber interior—a result of rays of light streaming through the marble panes—allowing you to peruse its sanctified holdings which include the Gutenberg Bible; manuscripts of Ezra Pound, H.D., Gertrude Stein, Edith Wharton, Langston Hughes, Richard Wright, and James Joyce; and Audubon prints. The centerpiece, a six-story book tower, presides over an underground working library illuminated by light streaming through a sunken court that features sculptures by Isamu Noguchi representing the earth, the sun, and chance.

In the quadrangle stands the Ledyard Flagstaff, erected in memory of Augustus C. Ledyard, who was killed in action in the Philippine Islands in 1899. Nearby is Alexander Calder's metallic **sculpture**, *Gallows and Lollipops* **[8]**.

★Bicentennial Buildings – Built to commemorate Yale's 200th anniversary in 1901, this group of buildings added an element of Beaux Arts classicism to the university's predominantly Gothic features. At right, **Woodbridge Hall** (Howells & Stokes, 1901), the small white limestone building of French Renaissance influence, houses the offices of the president and secretary of the university. Around

Michael Marsland /Yale University

Gallows and Lollipops by Alexander Calder

the top are carved the names of the founding trustees. Along the exterior wall of the **University Dining Hall** (Carrère & Hastings, 1901-02) is the Alumni War Memorial dedicated in 1927. One of the largest World War I memorials in the US, the massive colonnade boasts an architrave carved with the names of major battles. In front stands a cenotaph (empty tomb) decorated with military sculpture. The inscription echoes the words of Lincoln's "Gettysburg Address."

The rotunda, **Memorial Hall** (Carrère & Hastings, 1901-02), connects the dining hall with **Woolsey Hall** (Carrère & Hastings, 1901-02), the largest Yale auditorium and home of the New Haven Symphony Orchestra. Said to have inspired Yale student Maya Lin's design of the Vietnam War Memorial in Washington, the interior walls of Memorial Hall are inscribed with the names of over 1,000 Yale alumni who died in US wars, from the Revolution through Vietnam. The Civil War sculpture was designed by Henry Bacon, the architect of the Lincoln Memorial in Washington, DC.

Exit through the rotunda.

Look up Prospect Street to view the **Grove Street Cemetery** *(p 72)* and **Becton Engineering and Applied Science Center**, a striking concrete construction designed by Marcel Breuer & Associates. Completed in 1970 its oblong façade of precast panels is supported by piers that form an arcade along the sidewalk.

End of first walking tour. Continue to Hillhouse Avenue and Science Hill or return to the Yale Visitor Information Center. Turn right down College St. and continue to Elm St. passing the Elizabethan Club (No. 459). Turn left at Elm St. and continue to the Yale Visitor Information Center.

Hillhouse Avenue and Science Hill *Map opposite*

From the Visitor Information Center proceed down Elm Street and turn left on Temple St. Continue up Temple St. and turn left on Grove St. to Hillhouse Ave.

If continuing from the Central Campus tour, cross diagonally to Grove St. and Sheffield-Sterling-Strathcona Hall which houses the offices of Yale College and occupies the site of the old Yale Sheffield Scientific School (1861-1931) and Medical School (1813-60). Turn right on Grove St. and continue to Hillhouse Ave. Turn left on Hillhouse and continue up the street.

St. Mary's Church – Completed in 1870, this Gothic structure (James Murphy, 1870-76) ranks as the oldest Roman Catholic Church in New Haven; its interior boasts clustered piers and foliated capitals. The fraternal order of the Knights of Columbus was established here in 1881.

■ Farmington Canal

Between Musical Instruments and Health Services *(17 Hillhouse Ave.)* lies the Farmington Canal, constructed in the 1820s to extend from the New Haven harbor through Farmington, Connecticut, to Northampton, Massachusetts. For two decades, until a railroad took its place, the canal facilitated the economic development of New Haven and the state's inland towns and provided a popular system of transportation and recreation for its residents.

Yale Collection of Musical Instruments – *Description p 63.*

From the intersection of Hillhouse and Trumbull look up the avenue deemed in the 19C by Charles Dickens, "the most beautiful street in America." Continue up the avenue past the grand 19C Greek Revival, Italianate, and Victorian Gothic mansions now housing Yale administrators and departments.

No. 24 – The only residence remaining on the lower block of Hillhouse Avenue, this National Historic Landmark is a fine example of the Italianate style of New Haven's most famous architect, Henry Austin. Completed in 1849 for geology

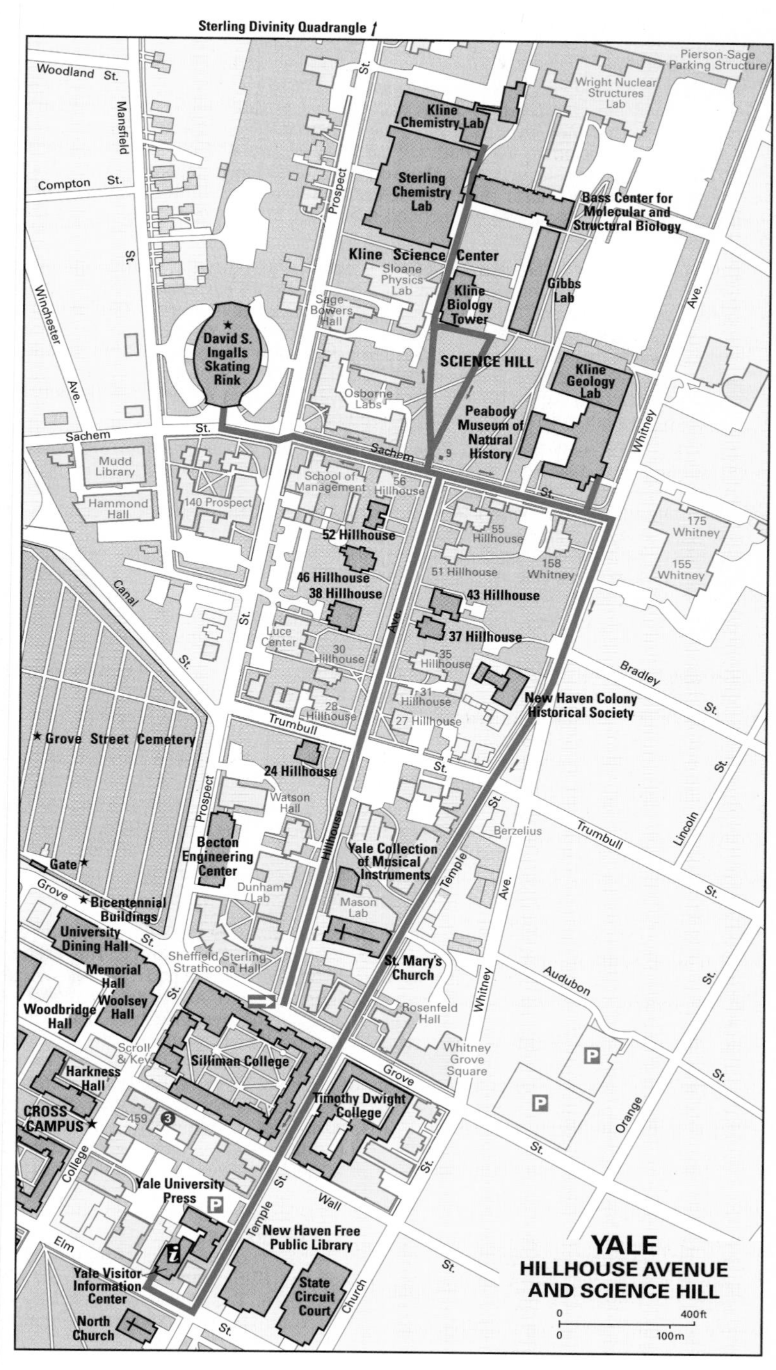

professor James Dwight Dana, it adjoins the **Farmington Canal** cut. Its formal cube-like appearance is enlivened by the contrasting dark trim of the wide-bracketed roof windows and porch. Note the columns carved with unusual plant motifs. Today it houses the Department of Statistics.

Cross Trumbull St.

No. 37 – This light brown Italian villa constructed in 1866 is of special historical interest due to its former occupants. The great American educator Professor **Daniel Coil Gilman** lived here in the early 1870s before going west to serve as president of the University of California. Later he became the first president of Johns Hopkins and of the Carnegie Institution. **George Bush** ('48) lived here with his wife and baby son George W. ('68) when the house was used as a residence for married students after World War II. It currently provides offices for the economics department.

No. 38 – Now the Office of Undergraduate Admissions, this two-story Beaux-Arts Revival mansion completed in 1892 was the last private residence constructed on the avenue. Designed by Bruce Price—the fashionable architect of society hotels and mansions, including the Château Frontenac in Quebec City—the home marked a return of the classical style to the avenue. Handsomely decorated with Grecian banded designs and floral embellishments in the iron work, the house also boasts horizontal stone bands that are echoed next door in the 1995 construction Henry R. Luce Hall.

No. 43 – Home of Yale presidents since 1937, this unique house was originally designed in 1870 for the wealthy railroad builder Henry Farnam in a High Victorian Gothic style by Russell Sturgis, Jr. In the 1930s when Farnam's bequest to the university was about to become the permanent home for Yale presidents, the style was unfashionable, and the house was remodeled into a Georgian Revival residence with a red-brick facade. Traces of its former Gothic glory as the finest house on the avenue remain; see especially the wing over the porte cochere on the side. The parklike grounds extend to Whitney Avenue.

No. 46 – The most imposing Greek Revival house on the avenue, attributed to Ithiel Town and Alexander Jackson Davis, this colonnaded two-story structure was built c.1839 for Aaron Skinner, Class of 1823, who conducted a boys boarding school here and later served four terms as mayor of New Haven. After his death in 1858, it was purchased by William Whiting Boardman, Class of 1812, a wealthy politician. In 1908 it was purchased by the Trowbridge family. This last privately owned residence on the avenue was bequeathed to Yale by Rachel Trowbridge in 1983. An elevated site and four large ionic columns contribute to its majestic quality. Be sure to peek around the back at its charming formal garden. The house is now the International Center for Finance, School of Management.

No. 52 – The Italian villa style assumed new heights in this 1849 towered design also by Henry Austin. The house was constructed for John Pitkin Norton, benefactor of the Amistad captives *(p 70)* and a founder of the Yale Sheffield Scientific School, who died a few years later at the age of 30. Purchased by Yale in 1923, it served as the first home of the Drama School, the Yale Psycho-Clinic, the Center for Alcohol Studies, and in 1977 it was assigned the School of Management.

Hillhouse Avenue quickly returns to the 20C at Sachem Street with the striking view of Roy Lichtenstein's 31ft-high steel sculpture *Modern Head* **[9]** (1974, 1989). The sculpture was installed in 1993 to commemorate the inauguration of Yale President Richard C. Levin (Ph.D. '74). North of Sachem Street is **Science Hill**.

Cross Sachem St. and turn left. Continue down Sachem St. crossing Prospect St.

★**David S. Ingalls Skating Rink** – *For daily schedules ☎ 203-432-0875.* One of the most distinguished collegiate hockey facilities in the country, the arena is named in honor of David S. Ingalls ('20) who twice captained the Yale hockey team, and his son David Jr. ('56) who served as captain of his freshman and varsity teams. Completed in 1958, this unique skating arena designed by Eero Saarinen *(p 36)* features a 300ft-long curved arched roof. Called a turtle, fish, or upside-down Viking ship because of its unusual shape, it is popularly known as "The Yale Whale." The rink is notable in the history of architecture as one of the first modern architectural designs to break from the rigid cubelike forms that had characterized modern architecture since the 1930s. During construction, when Saarinen first saw the 300ft central concrete arch of the rink rise above campus in the fall of 1957, he said it looked "like the spine of a giant dinosaur." The rink, which has nearly 3,000 seats, is made of concrete with an aluminum roof supported by cables. Beneath the arched roof, 76ft high at its zenith, hangs a wood ceiling suspended by cables that was designed to provide good acoustics for the facility. Ingalls also contains a weight room, three locker rooms, and a reception room, which houses Yale team photos dating back to 1895. Home games of the Yale men's and women's hockey teams are played here. The rink is also used by the Figure Skating Club, intramural hockey, Yale Youth Hockey, and for recreational skating by the community.

Michael Marsland /Yale University

David S. Ingalls Skating Rink

Return to Sachem St. and retrace your steps crossing Prospect St. back to the intersection of Hillhouse Ave. and Sachem St. to Science Hill. Turn left at "Modern Head" and walk up to the plaza.

Kline Science Center – The complex of buildings named after the major donor, pharmaceutical manufacturer C. Mahlon Kline ('01), was designed by Philip Johnson & Associates and completed in 1965. Dominating the elevated site formerly occupied by the Hillhouse family mansion and farm, Sachem's Wood, is the imposing 14-story Kline Biology Tower. Constructed of brick and brownstone in tubelike shafts that begin as massive columns and shrink into relief forms as they rise between the windows, the tower appears to be taller than its actual height. The tower houses research facilities, particularly for cellular biology; the subterranean Kline Science Library; and a cafeteria on the twelfth floor that offers sweeping views of the city and surrounding countryside. The Kline Chemistry Laboratory adjoins the Sterling Chemistry Laboratory, built northwest of the tower in the early 1920s. On the right side of the plaza lies the 1950s era Josiah Willard Gibbs Research Laboratories. In 1993 the buildings were connected at the north end of the plaza by the Bass Center for Molecular and Structural Biology. The Kline Geology Laboratory sits below Gibbs Lab next to the Peabody Museum on Whitney Avenue.

From the Osborn Memorial Laboratories (1914), up Prospect Street to Marsh Hall, a National Historic Landmark, and east to Whitney Avenue, the complex of buildings on **Science Hill** has grown. In addition to those described above there are facilities for physics, forestry, and environmental sciences. New additions to Science Hill will include four additional buildings for chemical, biological, and environmental research and for the School of Forestry and Environmental Studies. Adjacent to Science Hill a new facility for engineering will be built at the corner of Prospect and Trumbull Streets.

Return to Sachem St. and turn left. Continue on Sachem St. to the intersection of Whitney Ave.

Peabody Museum of Natural History – *Description p 62.*

Upon exiting the museum proceed down Whitney Ave. crossing Sachem St.

Continue on Whitney Avenue past the **New Haven Colony Historical Society** *(p 74)*. Proceed down Temple Street past undergraduate residential colleges **Silliman** and **Timothy Dwight**. On the right is the **Yale University Press** *(No. 302)*. At the corner of Temple and Elm is the **New Haven Free Public Library** *(p 69)*. Turn right on Elm Street to return to the Visitor Information Center.

★★ STERLING MEMORIAL LIBRARY

For 70 years, the Sterling Memorial Library has been a major force, attracting research materials and scholars and stimulating their interaction in an inspirational setting. When the library honoring Yale benefactor John William Sterling, Class of 1864, was completed in 1930 it was one of the largest in the world, providing a shelf capacity for three million volumes and seating for two thousand readers. As the library collection has grown to over ten million volumes in twenty-one libraries, Sterling now serves as the central research library for the humanities.

Visit *1 hr.*

Rose Walk, 120 High St. Open year-round Mon–Thu 8:30am–midnight, Fri 8:30am–5pm, Sat 10am–5pm & Sun 1pm–midnight. Hours may vary during summer sessions and school breaks. www.library.yale.edu. ☎ 203-432-2798.

The most technologically advanced structural and mechanical features were incorporated in this masterpiece of modern Gothic architecture designed by James Gamble Rogers. Constructed of varying hues of granite and Indiana limestone, the massive cathedral-like structure is dominated by the 15-story bookstack tower. On top of the tower sits the elaborately decorated metallic structure known as the castle. The library is lavishly decorated to illustrate the histories of books, writing, and Yale, in sculpture by Lee Lawrie and Rene P. Chambellan, stained glass windows by G. Owen Bonawit, and ironwork by Samuel Yellin. Over the main entrance, sculpture depicts ancient civilizations based on their written records, comprised of two groups of five panels separated by a large figure of a Medieval scholar. Below the writings are scribes associated with each culture.

Enter the **main entrance hall** called the nave. The 10 stone panels below the large windows on the sides of the Hall represent scenes from the history of the Yale Library in chronological order from the first bay on the left and then across to the right:

1701 – the founding of the college and the library

1714 – Jeremiah Dummer's gift of books

1718 – the removal of the library from Saybrook

1718 – Commencement in New Haven

1732 – Bishop Berkeley's gift to Yale

1742 – the first catalog by President Clap

1753 – the founding of the Linonia Society

1768 – the founding of Brothers in Unity (student literary clubs)

1779 – British invasion of New Haven

1865 – Daniel Coit Gilman resigning as Librarian

In the windows above the panels are eighty stained glass panes depicting scenes in the history of New Haven and Yale. In back of the carved oak circulation desk is a mural by Eugene Savage of Alma Mater receiving gifts from Light, Truth, Science, Labor, Music, Fine Arts, Divinity, and Literature. To the left is the recently renovated **Starr Main Reference Room**. Be sure to look for the whimsical carvings of a mop and pail, whiskbroom and scrub brush over a door by the reference room. To the right is the new **Irving S. Gilmore Music Library**, one of the largest in its field in the US. Constructed within the library's **light court**★ is a spectacular four-story-high vaulted ceiling supported by six large metal trusses.

Continue through the **Cloister Hall** overlooking the library courtyard and fountain. Twelve corbels on both sides of the hall informally portray readers and students napping, smoking, drinking, listening to a crystal set radio, and reading a humorous book, "U. R. A. JOKE." At the end of the hallway on the left is the **Memorabilia Room**, where archival material and artifacts from the collections of Manuscripts and Archives relating primarily to the history of Yale are exhibited. On permanent display are a model of the Yale campus displayed at the 1904 World's Fair in St. Louis, a large oil painting of the **Yale Fence** and students in 1888, and two sections of the historic Yale Fence. Turn back and enter the library courtyard, a picturesque garden spot for reading and relaxation. The lead fountain in the center was made in England from antique molds. Exit through the door near the main entrance.

Michael Marsland /Yale University

★ The Yale Bowl

2.5mi west of the Yale Visitor Information Center. From the New Haven Green go west on Chapel St. passing the Hospital of St. Raphael then a slight left onto Derby Ave. The Bowl is on the right at 251 Derby Ave. The Yale Bowl opened on November 21, 1914, for the Yale-Harvard game and has been the site of 497 college football games, two seasons of NFL action, and was the main venue for the 1995 Special Olympic World Games. The NFL's New York Giants and Detroit Lions brought professional football to the Bowl for their historic first meeting in 1960. The Giants, who played the New York Jets in a number of memorable exhibition contests during the 70's, used the Bowl as their home field in 1973 and 1974 while Yankee Stadium was being renovated.

Charles A. Ferry, Class of 1871, proposed the design for the Yale Bowl. Work began on the project in August 1913, with 145 men working for the Sperry Engineering Company of New Haven. The portals were constructed first, then the excavation began. Once the 30ft walls were formed to support the top rows of seats, the nearly thirty miles of wooden-backed seats were put in place. The cost of the final product: $750,000. The Bowl is 930ft long and 750ft wide, covering 12 1/2 acres. More than 320,000 cubic feet of earth was moved to form the bowl and the stadium now contains 22,000 cubic yards of concrete and 470 tons of steel.

In constructing the Bowl, dirt and rock were scooped out with amazing speed and piled high around the excavation to support the above-ground bleachers. The surplus was used to fill 12 acres of swamp between the Bowl and the West River. The Bowl was located so that the afternoon sun would not shine in the eyes of the football players. To convey the enormous quantity of concrete required for the walls, stone benches, and the 30 small and two large entrance tunnels, track for a railway was laid around the interior of the Bowl. The concrete, prepared in a factory erected at the site, was carried by a chute from a high tower down to horse-drawn cars on the track below. The capacity of this National Historic Landmark is 64,269 (it was 70,869 before alterations) and every seat has an unobstructed view of the playing field. After 85 years, the concrete structure of the Yale Bowl is in need of some repair and plans are underway to restore this marvel of 20C engineering.

ADDITIONAL SIGHTS

Medical Campus – *333 Cedar St.* The medical campus comprises the Schools of Medicine and Nursing. Yale's fastest-growing segment, the medical school represents about half the university's budget and, together with the Yale-New Haven Hospital and St. Raphael's Hospital, is the generator of a growing number of medical and biotechnology-related jobs in the area. Adjoining the medical school on Cedar Street is its primary teaching hospital, the Yale-New Haven Hospital, a 900-bed facility ranked among the best hospitals in the US. Staffed by 2,500 university-based and community physicians practicing more than 100 medical specialties, Yale-New Haven, in conjunction with the medical school and the Yale Cancer Center, is nationally recognized for its commitment to teaching and clinical research. In recent years, the formal Georgian Revival campus dating from the 1920s has been greatly expanded and enriched with buildings by distinguished modern architects. Some of the notable facilities include Philip Johnson's Laboratory of Epidemiology and Public Health (1963), Frank O. Gehry's and Allan Dehar's Yale Psychiatric Institute (1990), and Cesar Pelli's Boyer Center for Molecular Medicine (1991).

Sterling Divinity Quadrangle – *409 Prospect St.* The beautiful Georgian Revival divinity school quadrangle situated on the northern heights of the campus was completed in 1932. Architects Delano & Aldrich modeled their design on Thomas Jefferson's University of Virginia, but it is more evocative of an 18C New England town. Constructed of handmade brick, the classically balanced grouping features three colonnaded pavilions on each side of a lawn that rises gently up to Marquand Chapel with its magnificent steeple. Founded in 1822, the divinity school was located prior to 1932 on the present site of Calhoun College.

“There is no intellectual or emotional substitute for the authentic, the original, the unique masterpiece.”

Paul Mellon

George, 3rd Earl Cowper, with the Family of Charles Gore (c.1775) by Johann Joseph Zoffany

Museums

YALE CENTER FOR BRITISH ART★★

Time: 2 1/2 hours. 1080 Chapel St.

Established by a gift of Paul Mellon, the Yale Center for British Art possesses the most comprehensive collection of British art outside Great Britain. Paintings, prints, drawings and rare books illustrate British life and culture from the 16C to the present with a special emphasis on works from the period between the birth of Hogarth (1697) and the death of Turner (1851).

The Moth and the Butterfly

Louis I. Kahn *(p 58)* succeeded in designing interior spaces that match the intimacy, warmth, and life characteristic of the works in the Mellon Collection. The building's simple exterior concrete frame filled with rectangular panels of pewter-finish steel and glass give rise to the description of the building as "the moth and the butterfly" since its gray panels seem to change mood with the sun. Two brightly lit courts form the core of the building, where natural light, admitted through a skylight roof, illuminates the interior space. Travertine marble, white oak, and natural linen wall coverings create a discreet and elegant backdrop for the exhibition of works of art. The entrance court provides a striking view up through the building's upper three floors, while the Library Court on the second floor is surrounded by the Reference Library, Print Room, and Rare Book Room.

Paul Mellon '29

Philanthropist and universal patron of the arts, Paul Mellon (1907-99) devoted much of his time and his fortune to bringing the arts to the American people. Best known for his stewardship of the National Gallery of Art in Washington, DC, he also established the Yale Center for British Art. Opposed to having the museum bear his name, Mellon hoped to encourage and inspire others to give. At his death, Paul Mellon was described by the *New York Times* as "the largest and most discerning donor that the American museum world has known in the second half of this century."
From the 1930s to the 1960s, Mellon assembled the finest and most comprehensive collection of British art outside of the national collection of British art at the Tate Gallery in London. In 1966 he donated to Yale his collection, including 1,300 paintings, 10,000 drawings, 20,000 prints, and 20,000 rare books, with the pledge of a building to house the collection and an endowment to sustain its operations in perpetuity. This generosity to his alma mater extended further to fund two residential colleges, entire courses of study, professorships, lectureships, and scholarships.

VISIT

Open year-round Tue–Sat 10am–5pm, Sun noon–5pm. Closed major holidays. Guided tours available. www.yale.edu/ycba. ☎ 203-432-2800. A floor plan can be obtained from the information desk. The Department of Rare Books and the Department of Prints and Drawings are open year-round Tue–Fri 10am–4:30pm. Prints, drawings, and rare books are accessible to visitors in the Study Room on the second floor. The Reference Library is open Tue–Fri 10am–4:30pm, and when the university is in session Sat 1pm–4:30pm. All of the library's holdings are searchable on the Yale on-line catalogue, ORBIS. Currently, 60,000 of the collection's 200,000 photographs have been catalogued in an on-line searchable database called FOCUS.

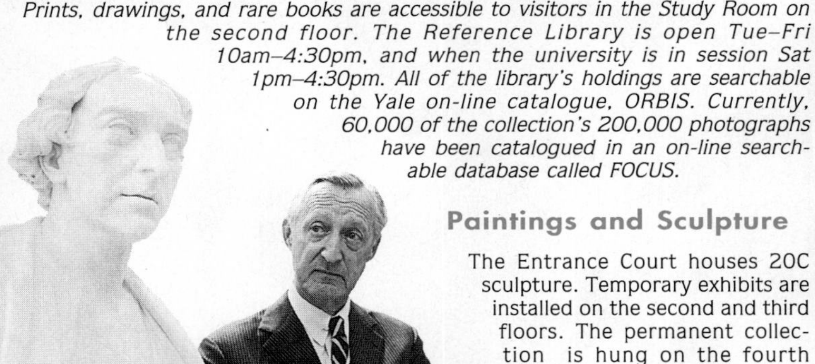

Courtesy of Yale Center for British Art

Paul Mellon

Paintings and Sculpture

The Entrance Court houses 20C sculpture. Temporary exhibits are installed on the second and third floors. The permanent collection is hung on the fourth floor.

16C to 18C – British painting in the 16C and early 17C shows a cautious but growing acceptance of the more sophisticated, realistic styles of European art. The most accomplished painters working in England were mainly imports from the Continent, particularly from the Low Countries. The visit to England of **Pe-**

ter Paul Rubens (1577-1640) in 1629 and the arrival of his most gifted pupil **Anthony van Dyck** (1599-1641) at the court of Charles I in 1631 changed the course of British painting.

William Hogarth (1697-1764) is generally credited as the first major British-born painter. He was by trade an engraver and achieved fame through his series of prints such as *The Rake's Progress* and *The Harlot's Progress*. He brought the same sense of earthy reality to portraiture and genre painting.
The conversation piece, one of the most characteristic genres of 18C British painting, takes the form of a group portrait, most frequently of members of the same family. Works by **Charles Phillips** (1708-47) and Hogarth at the beginning of the 18C, through **Arthur Devis** (1711-87) in the middle years, to a final flowering in the art of **Johann Zoffany** (1733-1810) and **Frances Wheatley** (1747-1821) represent the evolution of the genre.
The Grand Tour—with Italy as the final goal—was almost an obligatory part of a British artist's education. **Richard Wilson** (1713-82) began as a portrait painter, went to Italy in 1750, and fell under the spell of the Italian landscape and the classical landscape painting of **Claude Lorrain**.
For **Joshua Reynolds** (1723-1792) the experience of working in Rome from 1752 to 1754 was critical to the whole of his career; he was a painter determined to elevate portraiture from mere "face-painting" to the Grand Manner of High Renaissance art.

William Hogarth	*The Beggar's Opera*	1729
Joshua Reynolds	*Mrs. Abington as Miss Prue in `Congreve's Love for Love'*	1771
Peter Paul Rubens	*Peace Embracing Plenty*	1633-34
Anthony van Dyck	*Mountjoy Blount, 1st Earl of Newport*	c.1637-38

The Grand Tour was not the only way for British artists to achieve fame and standing. **Thomas Gainsborough** (1727-88), Reynolds's greatest contemporary and rival, never went to Italy. His early work shows the strength Gainsborough derived from the English landscape, frequently setting his figures down in familiar places—bringing out the "natural man" in his portraits, the reverse of Reynolds' Grand Manner.

Joseph Wright of Derby (1734-97) visited Italy in 1773 even though he had already established his reputation through his luminous evocations of the power of the antique and the spectacle of industry. Depicting scenes at night as though lit from a single mysterious source, and at the same time celebrating scientific innovations, Wright of Derby was the quintessential painter of the Enlightenment.
The greatest British painter of animals, **George Stubbs** (1724-1806) spent his early career in York working as a portrait painter. From about 1760 Stubbs established himself in London as a painter of racehorses, hunting scenes, and various animal subjects, attracting eminent aristocratic patrons. In the mid 1770s he began collaborating with the famous master potter Josiah Wedgwood—painting family portraits, modeling relief plaques and developing ceramic tablets on which to paint enamel.

Canaletto	*Warwick Castle*	c.1748-49
Thomas Gainsborough	*John and Ann Gravenor, with their Daughters*	c.1752-54
George Stubbs	*Zebra*	1763
Richard Wilson	*Dinas Bran from Llangollen*	1770-71
Joseph Wright of Derby	*Self-Portrait*	c.1780

19C and 20C – **John Constable** (1776-1837) was the first British painter to make a stand, as a matter of principle, against the classical ideal of landscape, in which nature is brought under strict aesthetic control, balanced, bathed in a warm atmosphere, and viewed from a height.
The progress of British landscape painting from mere record of place to vehicle of ideas reached its high point in the art of **Joseph Mallord William Turner** (1775-1851), the central figure in British Romantic painting.
The renegade Pre-Raphaelite Brotherhood, including the gifted **John Everett Millais** (1829-96), considered the Renaissance tradition of painting to have degenerated into artificiality and disregard for nature. The leading figure in what is sometimes called the "Aesthetic Movement" was the American-born **James McNeill Whistler** (1834-1903).

Dort or Dordrecht: The Dort Packet-Boat from Rotterdam Becalmed (1818)
by J.M.W. Turner

Under the leadership of **Walter Sickert** (1860-1942), the **Camden Town Group** took its name from the tough, working-class district of north London where Sickert had his studio and found most of his subjects (*The Camden Town Murder*, c.1908). The more intellectual **Bloomsbury Group** comprised not only artists—**Vanessa Bell** (1879-1961) and **Duncan Grant** (1885-1978)—but also writers, including Bell's sister Virginia Woolf, and the critics Roger Fry and Clive Bell.
Since the 1920s British artists have played an ever more original and confident part in the international art world. **Ben Nicholson** (1894-1982) and **Barbara Hepworth** (1903-75) made the Cornish fishing village of St. Ives an important center of abstract art, while the painters of the School of London gave new energy to the tradition of figurative painting (**Francis Bacon**, *Study for the Head of a Screaming Pope*, 1952). An important sculptor of the modern age was **Henry Moore** (1898-1986), and the tradition of bold sculptural innovation among British artists has continued down to the "YBAs" (Young British Artists) of today, including **Damien Hirst** (b.1965) and **Rachel Whiteread** (b.1963).

Vanessa Bell	*Self-Portrait*	c.1915
John Constable	*Cloud Study*	1821
Damien Hirst	*In and Out of Love*	1991
John Everett Millais	*L'Enfant du Régiment*	1831-32
Ben Nicholson	*May 1955 (Gwithian)*	1955
J.M.W. Turner	*Staffa, Fingal's Cave*	1831-32
J.A.M. Whistler	*Nocturne in Blue and Silver*	1872-78
Rachel Whiteread	*Untitled (Ten Tables)*	1996

Prints and Drawings

With a collection of over 30,000 prints and 20,000 drawings, the Center's Department of Prints and Drawings offers a comprehensive survey of British graphic art from the exquisite jewel-like portraits by Elizabethan miniaturists such as **Nicholas Hilliard** (c.1547-1619) to vigorous drawings by contemporary artists of the School of London, **Frank Auerbach** (b.1931) and **Leon Kossoff** (b.1926). An in-depth representation of 18C and 19C watercolors allows visitors to follow the development of this distinctive school of painting. Leading watercolorists **Paul Sandby** (1725-1809), **John Robert Cozens** (1752-97), **Thomas Girtin** (1775-1802), and **J.M.W. Turner** (1775-1851) found in the medium a highly effective means of capturing the changing qualities of light and atmosphere in both native and exotic foreign landscapes. Noted artists **Thomas Rowlandson**, **Thomas Gainsborough**, **Samuel Palmer**, **Richard Parkes Bonington**, and **John Frederick Lewis** are also well represented. A highpoint is the extensive collection of the art of the visionary poet, painter, and printmaker, **William Blake** (1757-1827). Also of interest are the sporting prints, caricatures, topographical prints, and architectural drawings.

Fans of 20C art will be thrilled with one of the largest groups of drawings and watercolors by **Augustus** and **Gwen John** outside the United Kingdom. The collection of modern printmaking ranges from the work of **Walter Sickert** at the beginning of the century, through works by **Graham Sutherland**, **David Hockney**, **Eduardo Paolozzi**, and **Lucian Freud**, to the latest productions by **Damien Hirst**.

William Blake	*Jerusalem*	c.1804-20
John Robert Cozens	*Lake of Albano and Castel Gandolfo*	c.1783-5
Thomas Girtin	*The Abbey Mill Knaresborough*	c.1801
Leon Kossoff	*Christ Church, Spitalfields, No. 2*	1990
Paul Sandby	*View of Windsor*	c.1765
J.M.W. Turner	*Mer de Glace*	1803

Rare Books and Archives

Housing approximately 20,000 volumes, the Department of Rare Books and Archives focuses on printed materials relating to the visual arts and cultural life in the United Kingdom and former British Empire from the 17C to the present.

The core of the collection of illustrated books is the Abbey Collection of 19C color-plate books that describe British life, customs, scenery, and travel, as well as hundreds of artists' manuals, dating from 1600-1900. Cartography enthusiasts will revel in the maps and atlases that led to *pax britannica*. **Christopher Saxon's** county atlas, **John Speed's** *Theater of the Empire of Great Britain*, **John Ogilby's** *Britannia*, **John Seller's** *English Pilot*, and **Des Barres'** *Atlantic Neptune* characterize the comprehensiveness of the collection. World travelers should not miss the earliest surviving manuscript of **Sir Francis Drake**'s circumnavigation (c.1587) of the globe. The extensive James Bruce archive contains journals, letters, drawings, and watercolors relating to his 18C expedition to discover the source of the Nile; books by **William Caxton** and other 15C and 16C printers; and 1,300 individual leaves from illustrated books printed before 1501; as well as a growing collection of contemporary artist books by **Ronald King** and **Ken Campbell**, among others. Archival material includes letters, journals, and account books by none other than **David Roberts**, **Dante Gabriel Rossetti**, **Edward Burne-Jones**, and **Vanessa Bell**.

Yale Center for British Art – Paul Mellon Collection

Jerusalem (c.1804-20) by William Blake

YALE UNIVERSITY ART GALLERY★★

Time: 2 hours. 1111 Chapel St.

A Calder cat, a Greek god, remarkable American silver, furniture, paintings and sculpture, and even a night on the town by van Gogh make for an enjoyable journey through the world's great works.

Historical Notes

Patriot artist John Trumbull's donation of his paintings to Yale marked the birth of the first university art gallery in the Western Hemisphere. Negotiated by his nephew-in-law, Benjamin Silliman, the acquisition of the collection assured that all students would have access to art and in turn established a new approach to art appreciation and education in the US. Originally housed in a building of classical influences designed by Trumbull himself, the collection moved to Street Hall constructed after New Havener Augustus R. Street, Class of 1812, and his wife, Caroline, donated the funds to establish the School of the Fine Arts. Yale's acquisition of the Jarves collection of Italian art in 1871 marked the beginning of the university's quest to expand its holdings. Today, the collection ranges from the 12C BC to the present, and its home is composed of two interconnected units: a 1928 building in the Gothic style, and the 1953 addition designed by Louis I. Kahn. His first major work, begun when the architect was 50 years old, the Gallery is considered Yale's first modern building. Its nondescript brick façade, concrete ceilings, and round stair tower provide a powerful yet graceful environment for displaying selections from the museum's 80,000-piece-collection.

■ Louis I. Kahn (1901-74)

Estonian-born and educated at the University of Pennsylvania School of Architecture, Kahn embraced the concept of well-ordered and defined spaces through the use of the wall and pier. His interior spaces, tapestries of structure and light, recall geometric form while allowing the building's purpose to dictate its design. Commissioned during his tenure at Yale (1947-57), Kahn's first notable design, the Yale University Art Gallery, sits across from his final work, The Yale Center for British Art, completed in 1977 after the architect's death.

VISIT

Open year-round Tue–Sat 10am–5pm, Sun 1pm–6pm. Closed major holidays. Contribution requested ($5). ♿ www.yale.edu/artgallery. ☎ 203-432-0600. Detailed floor plans are available at the Information Desk. Free guided tours available Sat 1:30pm & Sun 3pm. Sculpture Garden open year-round Tue–Sat 10am–4:30pm, Sun 1pm–6pm. For information on exhibits and activities, consult the Yale Art Gallery calendar, available in the lobby. The American galleries will be closed for reinstallation until early 2001.

Michael Marsland /Yale University

Yale University Art Gallery, Sculpture Hall

Ground Floor

Ancient Mediterranean art at Yale comprises more than 12,000 objects and spans 5,000 years, from the Neolithic period through the fall of the Roman Empire. The **Ancient Art** galleries feature art and artifacts from **Egypt**, the **Near East**, **Greece**, and **Rome.** Paintings, sculpture, and everyday objects such as fishhooks and leather shoes from the Yale-French excavations at the ancient city of **Dura-Europos** in Syria, brought to Yale in the 1930s, give a picture of life in this outpost on the eastern frontier of the Roman empire. Equally noteworthy are the stone, clay, and jade artifacts in the **Precolumbian** collection, featuring the art of the Olmecs, the Maya, the Aztecs, and the art of West Mexico.

First Floor

Special Exhibits, the McNeil Lecture Hall, McNeil Corridor, and Museum Shop are located on the first floor of the museum. Richard Serra's *Stacks*, a mural by Sol LeWitt, and Maillol's *L'Air* are on display in the Sculpture Hall. The Sculpture Garden can be accessed through the McNeil Corridor and from High Street.

Second Floor

11C to 19C European Painting and Sculpture – With special emphasis on 13C through 15C Italian panel paintings from Florence and Siena, the first section of the Gallery contains European art from the 11C to the early 16C. Highlights of the Jarves collection include rare 13C altarpiece panels while a significant portion of the collection is composed of examples from Tuscany, the epicenter of the early Renaissance, and more specifically Florence, where early 14C figures like **Dante** and **Giotto**, and **Petrarch** later in the century, ushered in the Italian Renaissance. The Medieval and Byzantine styles of severity and two-dimensionality gave way to figures rendered with heft and three-dimensional volume. This shift is most evident in the work of followers and contemporaries of Giotto such as **Bernardo Daddi**, **Taddeo Gaddi** and **Pacino di Bonaguida**. Another strength is the number of Sienese works from the early Renaissance. Works by the **Lorenzetti** and the Master of the Osservanza grace the walls with their intentionally abstract and old-fashioned style, quite unlike the art of Florence in the early 15C that was concerned with the employment of linear perspective to create naturalistic scenes. Finally, this section of the Gallery concludes in the late 15C and early 16C with works by **Veronese**, **Ghirlandaio**, **Pinturicchio**, **Francia**, and **Titian**.
The art of the Northern Renaissance is well represented with 16C paintings by **Cranach**, **Holbein**, **Breughel**, **Bosch** and **Marx Reichlich**, from overt Reformation art to works commissioned by wealthy, secular patrons. The 17C Dutch and Flemish art demonstrates the splendor of that golden age of painting by the likes of **Rubens**, **Hals**, **Goltzius**, and **Ruysdael**. The section of the Gallery of Italian, Spanish and French Baroque and Rococo art from the 17C to the 18C includes works by **Rosa**, **Claude**, **Zurbaran**, **Fragonard**, **Tiepolo**, **Pater**, and **Robert**. Highlights of the 19C French Realism collection include works by **Courbet**, **Millet**, and **Manet**.

African Sculpture – Sculpture, primarily ritualistic masks and figures carved in wood, dominates the art of Africa. Objects on display evidence the tremendous variety of shapes, proportions and designs present in African sculpture. Among the fine pieces that may be on display are initiation masks, woman-and-child images created as icons of human perfection and fertility, and reliquary guardian figures.

Third Floor

Late 19C European and Contemporary Art – The Gallery is divided chronologically beginning with Impressionism and ending with contemporary artists such as **Jasper Johns**. Yale's undisputed masterpiece, the *Night Café* by van Gogh, hangs as the centerpiece of the area containing works of Impressionism, Post-Impressionism, Primitivism, Expressionism, Futurism, Cubism and other early works of Modernism. Highlights include works by **Renoir**, **Monet**, **van Gogh**, **Picasso**, **Braque** and **Kandinsky**. The area near the elevators links this section to later art and contains works representative of the Dutch De Stijl movement by artists such as **Mondrian**.
Works given by Katherine Dreier as a part of the Collection Société Anonyme include creations by **Duchamp**, **Man Ray**, and **Ernst**. Paintings by **Kline**, **Motherwell**, **Rothko**, **Johns**, **Lichtenstein**, and **Warhol**, as well as **Pollock**'s *Arabesque*, highlight the post-war collection.

American Art – The collections of American paintings, sculpture, and decorative arts span more than three centuries; they occupy the eastern wing of the third floor and are organized chronologically as well as thematically.

Early 19C to mid-20C Paintings and Sculpture – The sense of optimism and abundance that characterized American culture in the first half of the 19C is seen in the glowing landscapes of **Thomas Cole** (1801-48), considered the father of the Hudson River School of landscape painters who flourished between 1820 and 1880, and whose shared esthetic was to sketch directly from nature. Though their interests ultimately ranged far beyond the Hudson River Valley, the river and its bordering mountains remained among their favorite subjects. Some artists recorded nature, others interpreted it, yet they all believed that the most distinctive and impressive characteristic of American scenery was its wilderness.

Among the important "first generation" of landscape artists were **Frederic E. Church** (1826-1900) and **Sanford Gifford** (1823-80) followed by later artists such as **Albert Bierstadt** (1830-1902), renowned for his vast monumental and panoramic landscapes of the American West, and **Martin Johnson Heade** (1819-1904), recognized for his sensitive marsh views and dramatic paintings of orchids and hummingbirds in a tropical landscape.

The mid-19C also saw the rise of American sculpture, largely due to the efforts of a group of sculptors who settled in Italy, expressly to learn and pursue their art in marble. The white marble works of such artists as **Hiram Powers** and **Horatio Greenough** embodied ancient Greek ideals of perfection, and were influenced by the Classical Revival in America. **Powers'** *The Greek Slave*, the first Neoclassical sculpture created by an American, was recognized internationally, and served as an artistic breakthrough against the repressiveness of Victorian mores.

Following the Civil War (1861-1865) many artists turned to a more personal expression, among them the evocative genre scenes of **Winslow Homer** (1826-1910) and the interiorized portraits by **Thomas Eakins** (1844-1916), two artists considered by many to be the greatest American artists of the 19C. The paintings and sculpture of the Collection Société Anonyme, founded by Duchamp, Ray, and Dreier in 1920 to introduce contemporary European art to the American public placed Yale in the forefront of modern collecting. It includes substantial holdings by native or adoptive Americans such as **Joseph Stella** (1877-1946), **Patrick Henry Bruce** (1881-1936), **Arshile Gorky** (1904-1948), and **John Covert** (1882-1960). The modernist paintings of **Charles Sheeler** (1883-1965) combined his interest in early American handicraft, especially that of the Shakers, with the sharp edges and clearly defined planes of contemporary photography. Regarded as one of the most "American" of artists in the 1920s was **George Bellows** (1882-1925)—he did not study abroad and was little influenced by European Modernism—whose paintings are characterized by assertive brushwork and a youthful vigorousness. Sheeler's and Bellows' contemporary **Edward Hopper** (1882-1967) focused on the transience of American life in the mid-20C, and his mastery of light and form to create mood are clearly seen in his paintings of a motel room, a cafeteria, and an empty room.

Trumbull Gallery – Late 17C and 18C portraits, miniatures, and history paintings are installed to convey the impression of a 19C picture gallery. Agrippina, a monument of Neoclassicism by **Benjamin West** (1738-1820), and the original series of scenes from the American Revolution by **John Trumbull** (1756-1843) are among its most notable holdings. Applying West's and **John Singleton Copley**'s realistic innovations in European history painting to American subjects, Trumbull created a series of images that have become icons of American nationalism of which *The*

The Declaration of Independence, 4 July 1776 (1787-1820) by John Trumbull

Declaration of Independence is perhaps the most well-known painting in American art. Like British painting of the 18C and early 19C, American art focused on portraiture in the Grand Manner. Eminent artists of this period include **Charles Willson Peale** (1741-1827), **John Singleton Copley** (1738-1815), and **Gilbert Stuart** (1755-1828), who was sometimes called the "court portraitist to the young Republic" because of his many paintings of early leaders. The remarkable portrait miniature collection dates from around 1760 to 1830, the heyday of miniature painting, and includes the major miniaturists of the time—**John Ramage**, **Charles Fraser**, and **Edward Greene Malbone.**

Late 18C to mid-20C Decorative Arts – The strength of the Gallery's American decorative arts lies in the Colonial and early Federal periods. The Francis P. Garvan (Class of 1897) collection of decorative arts is representative of early American history. Early **silver** contains rare objects, as for example the monteith bowl (c.1705) by Boston silversmith **John Coney.** Yale's **furniture** collection comprises outstanding examples of 17C, 18C, and early 19C pieces, including the renowned six-shell blockfront **desk** and bookcase made in Rhode Island about 1765 for the Providence merchant John Brown. In addition to the furniture displayed in the Art Gallery, more than 1,000 examples can be seen by appointment in the Garvan Furniture Study. Also part of the American decorative arts are significant holdings in glass, for example a rare presentation tumbler made in 1789 in Maryland by **John Frederick Amelung**. The pewter collection boasts unique examples, such as the flagon made by **Henry Will** in New York sometime between 1761 and 1793. The major manufacturers of early American ceramics, such as **William Ellis Tucker** who worked in Philadelphia between 1826 and 1838, are also represented. Since the 1970s Yale has been acquiring late 19C and 20C objects to establish a comprehensive collection representative of a variety of artists, styles, forms, time periods, and regions that includes works by the firm of **Herter Brothers** and **Frank Lloyd Wright**.

Monteith Bowl by John Coney

Mabel Brady Garvan Collection /Yale University Art Gallery

1950 to present Decorative Arts – Holdings include work by Dale **Chihuly**, **Saarinen**, **Gehry**, and **Venturi**, as well as mass-produced furniture and tableware. Don't miss the costume jewelry by Mary **McFadden** and Elsa **Freund**. The **Branford rooms: recreation from a Colonial Connecticut house** will be newly installed with interpretive displays of American life in the 18C, from "food-ways" objects related to the preparation of food to the service and consumption of food.

Fourth Floor

Asian Art – Highlights of the Chinese holdings include ceramics from the Neolithic period (5000-3000 BC) through the Qing dynasty (AD 1644-1911); bronze ritual vessels; and paintings (Song dynasty, AD 960-1279, through contemporary). Of particular note are ceramics from the region of Changsha, Hunan Province. Buddhist art is represented by a Gandharan Seated Buddha, a Chinese stone stele (AD 6C), a Chinese polychrome wood image of Guanyin (AD 1168), and a Japanese wooden image of Taishakuten (AD 10C). Japanese art can be seen in 17C folding screens; late 17-19C polychrome woodblock prints; and contemporary ceramics. Installations rotate two to three times a year.

Prints and Drawings – Trace the history of the graphic arts by way of 25,000 prints, 6,000 drawings, and 3,000 photographs dating from the 15C to the 20C. Rotating exhibits display selections from a collection especially strong in 16C and 17C Dutch and Flemish drawings, 19C French drawings, prints and drawings of early modernism, and American art.

Michelin covers the USA with maps 491 Northeastern USA/Eastern Canada, 492 Southeastern USA and 493 Western USA/Western Canada.

PEABODY MUSEUM OF NATURAL HISTORY

Time: 2 hours. 170 Whitney Ave.

One of Connecticut's and Yale's most popular tourist attractions, the Peabody Museum serves as a crossroads for university research and public interest in the sciences. Collections of fossils, minerals, and artifacts of human cultures provide a better understanding of the region's as well as the world's innumerable wonders.

Historical Notes

The museum's collection dates to the 19C with Benjamin Silliman's appointment as professor of Chemistry and Natural History at Yale. Silliman's mineral collection, used as a teaching tool, became one of New Haven's most popular public attractions. In 1866, Yale alumnus Othniel Charles Marsh, nephew of the financier George Peabody, convinced his uncle to endow the university with funds for establishing a museum of natural history. Peabody's endowment of $150,000 allowed for construction of a building and the maintenance and expansion of the collection. That same year, Marsh was appointed the nation's first Professor of Paleontology. The collection found its Gothic Revival home designed by Charles Z. Klauder in 1924. Today the building houses more than 11 million specimens; exhibits range from towering dinosaurs to dioramas of animals shown in their natural habitats.

VISIT

Kids *Open year-round Mon–Sat 10am–5pm, Sun noon–5pm. Closed Jan 1, Easter Sunday, July 4, Labor Day, Thanksgiving Day, Dec 24-25 & 31. Children ages 3-15 $3, adults $5. ♿ www.peabody.yale.edu ☎ 203-432-5050.*

First Floor – An awesome exhibition of prehistoric creatures installed in the **Great Hall** includes *Archelon*, the giant sea turtle, and the crowd-pleasing *Apatosaurus (Brontosaurus)*. Spanning the hall is Rudolph F. Zallinger's Pulitzer Award-winning mural, *The Age of Reptiles*, which vividly summarizes over 300 million years of animal and plant evolution. In the **Hall of Mammalian Evolution** next door, don't miss the saber-toothed cat, a 11,000-year-old ground sloth, and, a second Zallinger mural, *The Age of Mammals*. Other exhibits explore the cultural practices of indigenous peoples from the New World, Southeast Asia, and Oceania.

Upper Floors – Kids and kids at heart head to the **Discovery Room** *(Mon–Fri 10am–3pm, Sat 10am–5pm, Sun noon–5pm)* to engage in some hands-on fun and to get a good **view** of the Great Hall. Exhibits in the **Silliman Hall of Rocks and Minerals** feature the geology of Connecticut as well as minerals of New England and Eastern New York. **Dioramas** by master painters J. Perry Wilson and Francis Lee Jaques illustrate aspects of the natural world from New England and North America. In the **Hall of Connecticut Birds** you'll find a majority of the state's species. Next to the exhibit on Connecticut's Native Americans, and almost equal in appeal to the dinosaurs, is **Ancient Egypt: Treasures of the Nile**.

Peabody Museum of Natural History /Yale University

The Age of Reptiles by Rudolph F. Zallinger

COLLECTION OF MUSICAL INSTRUMENTS

Time: 1 hour. 15 Hillhouse Ave.

Clavichords, harpsichords, pianos, wind and string instruments overwhelm you not only with the craftsmanship they exhibit but also the roles they have played in the evolution of one of the most popular forms of human enjoyment. See the instruments that shape our understanding of music.

Historical Notes

The Collection was established in 1900 when Morris Steinert, a local piano retailer, donated portions of his private collection of antique stringed and keyboard instruments to Yale. Over the next half century, these 45 instruments were supplemented by individual gifts from alumni and occasional purchases at large. Acquisitions of the Belle Skinner Collection of Old Musical Instruments (1960), the Emil Herrmann Collection of Historical String Instruments (1962), and the Robyna Neilson Ketchum Collection of Bells (1974) considerably enhanced the holdings. In 1960, the collection moved to the former home of Alpha Delta Phi, a two-story, red sandstone Richardsonian structure (1894) designed by W.H. Allen. More than an exhibit of exquisite instruments, the Collection serves as a working laboratory for students, restores and maintains the instruments in playable condition, and provides concerts to the public.

VISIT

Open Sept–Jun Tue–Thu 1pm–4pm. Closed Jul & Aug, university recesses. ☎ 203-432-0822. Concert Info ☎ 203-432-0825. Please note that not all instruments are on display at any given time. A series of five or six concerts is presented on Sunday afternoons in the Gallery of Keyboard Instruments. Specialists in the performance of music in its historical context are featured playing restored instruments from the museum's collections. Calendars for the series are available on request.

Harpsichord (1770) by Pascal Taskin

Susan Thompson/Yale Collection of Musical Instruments /Yale University

A rare collection of more than 800 fine and decorative musical instruments document the European art music tradition from 1550 to 1900. Two permanent exhibits are supplemented regularly by the presentation of special exhibits. Violins by Jakob Stainer (1661) and Stradivari (1736), the famous violin maker of Cremona, and viols by Giovanni Battista Ciciliano (c.1550) and Pietro Guarneri (1689) are some highlights of the stringed instruments collection. Other significant pieces include an oboe by Jakob Denner (c.1720), a Joseph R. Bertet guitar made out of maple and walnut with a veneered ebony fingerboard and an exquisite four-tier parchment rose surrounded by ivory, ebony, and purfling; and guitars by Joachim Tielke (1702) and José Pernas (1843). On display in the **keyboard gallery★** is an outstanding array of instruments decorated with marquetry, sculpture and paintings, including spinetti by Annibale dei Rossi (1569) and Francesco Poggio (1620); harpsichords by Andreas Ruckers (1640), Johann Adolph Hass (c.1760), and Pascal Taskin (1770); and pianos by Koennicke (c.1795), Bösendorfer (1828), Broadwood (c.1842), Pleyel (1842), Bechstein (1864), Steinway (1867), and Erard (1881).

"We arrived at New Haven, where I was received with all Posible Respects and civility."

Sarah Kemble Knight's *Journal*, 1704

New Haven Green

New Haven

Yale 3

NEW HAVEN★★

Population 123,189
Map of Principal Sights p 6
Tourist Office ☎ 203-777-8550 or www.newhavencvb.org

Quaint commercial districts, serene residential streets, the famous Green, (a great cemetery!), and landmarks of American history are only a few of the highlights of a place that has given the world the hamburger, the lollipop, and the corkscrew.

The Landscape

New Haven, with a land area of 21.2 sq mi and population of about 123,000, is the third largest city in Connecticut. Situated on the coastal plain, it has an official elevation of 33ft. The city meets the sea at its broad but shallow harbor at the confluence of the Quinnipiac, Mill, and West Rivers. Spanning the harbor is the Pearl Harbor Memorial Bridge, known as the "Q" Bridge, on Interstate 95, at the southern terminus of Interstate 91. Still visible behind the downtown skyline are the city's major geographic landmarks, East and West Rocks. Both end in cliffs of a reddish brown hue, presenting an impressive view that is most spectacular at sunset. The color is produced by the combination of red sandstone and trap rock that has turned rust-colored due to the iron in the rock. New Haven is conveniently located 69 miles from New York City, 34 miles from Hartford, 85 miles from Providence, and 121 miles from Boston.

Historical Notes

The Quinnipiacks and the Puritans – At the time of the English settlement of New Haven in 1638, the Quinnipiacks, a small tribe of Native Americans, inhabited the area. Quinnipiack has been defined as "people from the long-water land" and also as "a turning point; to make a change in the direction of travel." Their population had been reduced to as few as 100 by disease and the wars of the aggressive neighboring tribes, the Pequots and the Mohawks. The plan to found a new colony in New England began in England in the 1630s when Puritans experienced great pressure to conform to the Anglican Church. In 1637, two devout Puritans, the Rev. John Davenport and his friend, Theophilus Eaton, a wealthy merchant, organized a group of 500 followers and sailed to America to carry out Davenport's mission to found "an independent kingdom of Christ," and a college to educate its leaders. The two shiploads of Puritans landed first in Boston. From there, Eaton's scouting party explored and selected for their settlement the large harbor and rich meadows of Quinnipiack. When the entire party followed in April 1638, the Quinnipiacks received the English in peace. In exchange for protection against the other tribes, the Quinnipiacks agreed to move to a 30-acre plot on the east shore of the harbor considered to be the first reservation for Native Americans in the US. Mostly well-to-do Londoners with little experience in farming, the settlers hoped to develop the colony into a prosperous trading center. There was little to trade, however, as fur pelts and minerals were scarce. A tragic event occurred in 1646, when a ship laden with goods and carrying some of the leading men of the town sailed from the harbor for England and was

never seen again. The entire community sank into a general depression until, according to folklore, one summer day a ghost ship appeared in the sky for all to see. They watched as the ship appeared to be torn apart and sunk by a violent gale. Taking this as a sign from heaven, the people found closure. Cotton Mather in *Magnalia Christi Americana* recorded the legend of the "Phantom Ship," and Longfellow wrote a poem about it. In addition to economic failures, the pressure that had forced the Puritans to flee England disappeared when the Puritans took control of England's government, and some settlers returned home. Of those who remained many expressed dissatisfaction with the authoritarian leadership of the elite few who governed the theocracy. To repress dissent, Governor Eaton's "Blue Laws" became even stricter, forbidding dancing, card playing, the celebration of Christmas, and most activities except prayer on the Sabbath.

The Regicides – After the Restoration of the English monarchy in 1660, New Haven's independent status was reduced. A new royal charter defined New Haven as a part of the colony of Connecticut whose capital was Hartford. One after another the colony towns of Branford, Guilford, Milford, Stamford (including Greenwich), and Southold, Long Island seceded, and on January 7, 1665 New Haven finally united with Connecticut. Two years later John Davenport, in despair over his failed mission, moved to Boston. During this period one of the most memorable series of events in local history took place. Two of the regicide judges who had signed the death warrant of King Charles I, (father of the new king James II), Col. Edward Whalley and his son-in-law Col. William Goffe, took refuge at the home of John Davenport in 1661. When the king's messengers reached New Haven to arrest them, the governor made them wait until the Sabbath was over. After they heard Davenport preach a sermon, "Hide the Outcasts," their search proved fruitless. The regicides were hidden in a cave at the top of West Rock, today a tourist site named "Judges Cave." For three years they lived in various parts of the New Haven Colony. Then in 1664 after another stay at the cave they went to Massachusetts where they were joined by a third regicide, Col. John Dixwell. Whalley soon died, and Goffe moved to Hartford where he died in 1680. Dixwell eventually came to New Haven where, under the pseudonym of James Davids, he was a successful member of the community and raised a family. After his death in 1689, he was buried on the Green, and his tombstone with the initials "J.D." may be visited behind Center Church. The three streets that begin together at Broadway and extend toward West Rock are named after the regicides: Whalley Avenue, Goffe Street, and Dixwell Avenue.

Benedict Arnold, Local Hero – Through the rest of the 17C, New Haven remained largely an agricultural town, with its spacious Green, or marketplace at the center. In 1701, New Haven, already a county seat, was designated a co-capital of the colony with Hartford. When the governor and General Assembly met in New Haven for the first time in October they passed "An Act for Liberty to Erect a Collegiate School." The first site in Saybrook, at the mouth of the Connecticut River, proved to be unsatisfactory, and in 1716 it was decided to move the school to New Haven. By the middle of the 18C, the local economy began to thrive as shipping increased. In 1755, the first newspaper in the state, *The Connecticut Gazette*, began publication in New Haven. By 1775, the town with a population of about 3,500 became fully committed to achieving independence from England thanks to the efforts of Benedict Arnold. When

Nate Leigh

the news of the Battle of Lexington reached New Haven on April 21, 1775, the local militia, under the command of Benedict Arnold, voted to march to assist their fellow patriots in Massachusetts. The next day, Arnold assembled the men in full dress on the Green, where they received the blessing of the Rev. Jonathan Edwards, Jr. Marching up to Beer's Tavern, on the site of the Taft *(p 72)*, Arnold demanded of the selectmen the key to the king's powder. The selectmen still uncommitted to the revolutionary cause, held back. Arnold, shouting, "None but the Almighty God shall prevent my marching," persuaded them to turn over the key enabling him to claim the powder, ball and flint and march with his men to Boston. **Powder House Day**, the re-enactment of this historic event by the Second Company, Governor's Footguard, has been a yearly tradition in the Elm City since 1904.

Fortunately, New Haven had to be defended only once when British forces under Major General William Tryon briefly occupied and plundered it in 1779. After the war, New Haven planned for a new era by obtaining a city charter, in 1784, divesting itself of its surrounding agricultural towns, and concentrating on its commercial development. The first mayor was Roger Sherman, the only man to sign the Articles of Association, the Declaration of Independence, the Articles of Confederation, and the Constitution.

Innovation – Modern American manufacturing began at the outskirts of New Haven, in Whitneyville, now Hamden, in 1798. Shortly after his graduation from Yale in 1792, Eli Whitney transformed the Southern economy with his invention of the cotton gin. He then turned to the manufacture of guns using another of his innovations—calibrated interchangeable parts. On Whitney Avenue he built the nation's first factory village and proceeded to fill the first major US government arms contract for ten thousand muskets and bayonets. Whitney's production plan known as "the American System," was the prototype of modern manufacturing in New Haven and elsewhere. In the late 18C and early 19C, New Haven was an important seaport, participating mainly in the West Indian trade. In 1797 the *Neptune* set sail on a 32-month voyage around the world and returned with a cargo of silk, tea and chinaware producing profits of $240,000. Whaling and sealing were successful for a time, and later oystering became a profitable business. After the completion of the Erie Canal in 1825, construction of a waterway from the New Haven harbor north to Farmington and on to Northampton, Massachusetts began in the same year. From 1828 until 1846, when the Farmington Canal was replaced by a railroad, the canal operated at a financial loss, but it was highly beneficial to the New Haven economy providing new opportunities for inland trade. In addition to the railroad, coastal shipping of local and regional products became so active that on a single day in April 1855 fifty vessels were counted in the harbor.

Local inventions and improvements made New Haven a national center for the manufacture of hardware, carriages, corsets, rifles, and rubber footwear. **Samuel Colt** of the Whitney Arms Co. invented the automatic revolver in 1836. In 1867 the Winchester Repeating Arms Company opened, makers of the famous **Winchester** 73 rifle, "the gun that won the West." The most important industry in the city was carriage making, with the city boasting 18 factories in 1818 and 29 in 1872. Renowned among the makers of fine carriages was James Brewster. His carriages were especially popular in the South and were purchased by presidents Jackson and Van Buren. The advent of the automobile abruptly ended this major employment opportunity for the city.

The Elm City – Art and culture flourished in the 19C. James Hillhouse, the leading entrepreneur of the Federal period, instituted a beautification plan for the Green and the city, transforming the central square into the most pleasing in the country and leading to the opening of the historic Grove Street Cemetery in 1797. His plan for widespread planting of elm trees led to New Haven's nickname "The Elm City." Handsome mansions in the latest 19C styles replaced the simpler Georgian homes as an upper class of wealthy merchants, manufacturers, and entrepreneurs grew. These symbols of wealth and status appeared first on the portion of Elm Street facing the Green known as Quality Row, then around Wooster Square, and on Hillhouse Avenue dubbed by Charles Dickens, "the most beautiful street in America," and in the early 20C on Whitney Avenue, Prospect Street and the surrounding East Rock neighborhood.

Twentieth Century – About 1880, New Haven entered an era of rapid demographic change. The dominance of Congregationalists of English extraction eroded as large numbers of immigrants moved in, attracted by plentiful employment opportunities. While the Irish population dating from the building of the Farmington Canal continued to grow, the largest new groups were Italians and Russian Jews from Eastern and Southern Europe. Many Italians came to work in the Sargent Hardware Factory and settled nearby in and around Wooster Square. From 1900 to 1910, the city population swelled from 108,000 to 134,000, one third foreign-born, and another third second generation. The residential density in commercial areas led to the rise of slums and pollution that the City Beautiful reform movement in the early 20C was unable to stem. During this time Yale and New Haven grew apart physically and socially. Still, Yale provided an excellent avenue of upward mobility for residents as the tuition remained low and local students could live at home. While the city suffered through the Great Depression, its effect was alleviated by Yale's massive building program. Through the World War II era, affairs improved with the boom in government orders for arms and materiel especially at the Winchester Arms Company.

After 1945 the flight to the suburbs by residents and businesses continued to depress the city, but prospects improved in 1954 with the election of Mayor Richard C. Lee. Assisted by his development administrator Edward J. Logue and with the advice of Yale experts in planning and architecture, Lee received federal funds to finance a major redevelopment program. As one of the first cities to embark on such a massive renewal of its central core, New Haven was nationally known as "The Model City." In the cleared areas, businesses, apartment complexes, and a connector leading from Interstate 95 to downtown were built. The downtown area was also redeveloped by the mid-60s and featured an innovative indoor shopping mall, large department stores, and a hotel. Nevertheless, as with many northern cities, the manufacturing base continued to shrink. By 1970 the population had slipped from 160,000 in 1940 to 137,000, while Greater New Haven had grown from 246,000 to 356,000. The arts and culture however, have continued to thrive and enhance the city's importance as a major center of the arts. Greater New Haven's higher educational facilities include in addition to Yale, Albertus Magnus College, Gateway Community-Technical College, Quinnipiac University, Southern Connecticut State University, and the University of New Haven. In 1989, the city celebrated the 150th anniversary of the Amistad Affair and through the efforts of dedicated residents to educate the general public, the experience of the captives is now recognized as a milestone event in American history. As the official home port of the reproduction schooner built in Mystic Seaport, New Haven will continue to be the center of *Amistad* history events and tours.

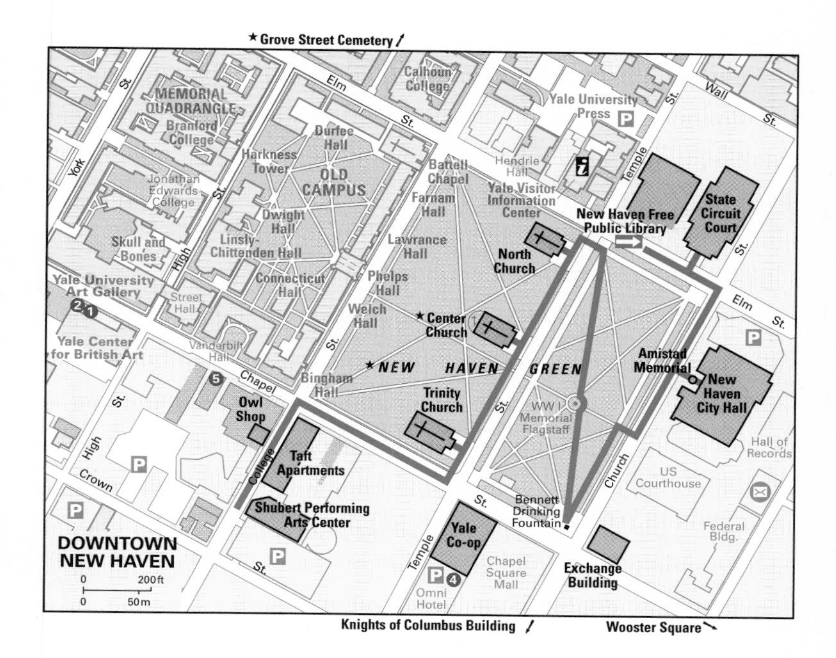

WALKING TOUR *2 hrs. Map above.*

Begin at the New Haven Free Public Library.

New Haven Free Public Library – *133 Elm St. Open year-round Mon–Thu 9am–9pm, Fri & Sat 9am-5pm, Sun 1pm–5pm. ☎ 203-946-8130.* Designed in 1908 by the noted architect Cass Gilbert, best known for the Woolworth Building in New York City as well as New Haven's Union Station, the brick and marble building was designed to harmonize with the traditional architecture of the churches on the Green. The building was formally dedicated to the City of New Haven on May 27, 1911. In 1990, a major renovation and expansion was completed with great care to preserve its Georgian Revival style.

State Circuit Court – *Corner of Elm and Church Sts.* Designed by William H. Allen and Richard Williams and completed in 1909, this Greco-Roman building exemplifies American Neoclassicism.

Turn right crossing Elm St. Continue down Church St.

Amistad Memorial – *165 Church St.* Completed by Ed Hamilton in 1992, this 14ft bronze sculpture pays tribute to the 53 Africans who escaped their slavery in 1839 by overpowering the Spanish crew of the ship *Amistad*. On the site stood the old New Haven Jail, in which the Africans were kept while awaiting trial. The unique, three-sided sculpture depicts aspects of the life of **Sengbe Pieh**, known as **Joseph Cinque**, the leader of the Amistad Captives.

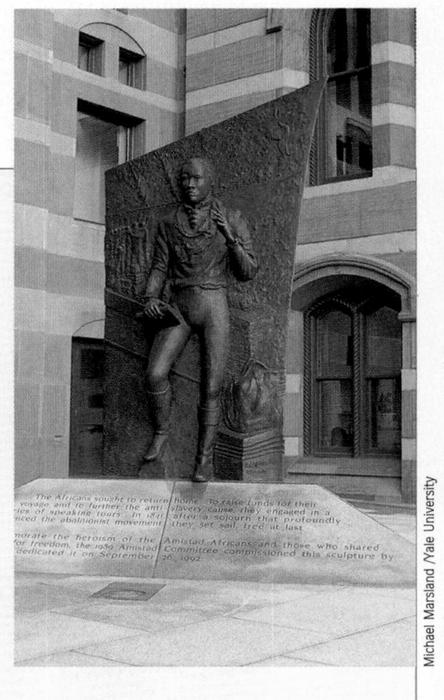
Michael Marsland /Yale University

■ The Amistad Affair, 1839-41

For over two years, New Haven was the focal point of the Amistad Affair, a major milestone in the long struggle to end slavery in the US. During those years a number of New Haven residents were actively involved in freeing and educating about 50 native Africans who were taken into slavery by Spaniards and sold in Havana. Aboard the ship *La Amistad*, the Africans under the leadership of Cinque overcame their captors and attempted to sail home. Their long odyssey to freedom was thwarted when, after two months of zigzagging north, they were taken into custody on Long Island and turned over to the nearest US Marshal, in New Haven. The defense attorney for the captives was **Roger Sherman Baldwin**, grandson of Roger Sherman. Yale professor **Josiah Willard Gibbs**, father of the famous physicist of the same name, gave the Africans a voice to defend themselves against charges of piracy and murder. After transcribing their Mende language phonetically, he searched the wharves of New York City until he found an African sailor who could serve as interpreter. Antislavery leaders aroused the public to join together to secure the freedom of the captives, raise funds to return them to their homeland, and promote the abolitionist cause. The great preacher and teacher **Leonard Bacon** wrote and lectured fervently on their behalf. Later, one of his notable phrases so impressed another antislavery champion, Abraham Lincoln, that he restated it in his famous declaration, "If slavery is not wrong, nothing is wrong." The freedom of the Africans was declared by courts in the Connecticut co-capitals, Hartford and New Haven, and affirmed in the US Supreme Court. Upon being set free, money was raised to charter a ship for the long voyage home. The Africans set sail in November 1841 and arrived in Sierra Leone in January. Other Amistad sites include a small permanent exhibit in the vestibule of Battell Chapel, and the reproduction schooner *Amistad*, scheduled to sail into New Haven harbor in summer 2000.

New Haven City Hall – *165 Church St.* This 1861 Henry Austin design features a brownstone Victorian Gothic façade. Look inside at the cast iron staircase, considered one of the finest High Victorian iron stairs in the US.

Between City Hall and the US Courthouse, cross Church St. to the Green. Walk left.

★**The Green** – The New Haven Green, a National Historic Landmark, has been the center of New Haven's civic life since 1638. Before it was bisected by Temple Street in 1784, the Green was one large square of the city's original nine squares. The lower Green, the east side with the flag pole, was marshy and unkempt and was even used to pasture cows until 1821. Later, markets and commercial fairs were held there, and today the lower Green is the site for concerts, rallies, and public events such as the Special Olympics World Games held in 1995. The upper Green, with the three churches, has been devoted to religious activities and, prior to 1875, governmental affairs. Behind Center Church, then called the Brick

Meeting-House, was the old burial ground with graves dating back to the earliest years of the settlement. The Green is carefully administered by a self-perpetuating body, the Proprietors of the Common and Undivided Lands of New Haven, dating from 1723.

Bennett Drinking Fountain – *Corner of the Green at Church and Chapel Sts.* The 1907 replacement for the old town pump, the drinking fountain was designed by the noted artist and dean of the Yale art school, John Ferguson Weir. It is modeled after the Athenian monument of Lysicrates. Note the drinking troughs for birds and animals.

Look past the Chapel Square shops to the left to view a New Haven landmark, the Knights of Columbus Building.

Knights of Columbus Building – *1 Columbus Plaza. Open year-round Mon–Fri 8am–4:30pm, by appointment only. ☎ 203-772-2130.* Affectionately called the "Tootsie Roll" building, the international headquarters of the Knights of Columbus was designed by Kevin Roche, John Dinkeloo and Associates and completed in 1967. The Knights of Columbus, founded in New Haven in 1882, is the world's largest organization of Roman Catholic men and their families. A distinctive feature of the New Haven skyline, the 23-story, glass-faced building is set off by four 320-ft, brown tile towers that symbolize the order's ideals of charity, unity, fraternity, and patriotism.

From the Green, look across Church St. to the building housing the Bank of Boston.

Exchange Building – *Intersection of Church and Chapel Sts.* Built in 1832, the Exchange was visible evidence of the new commercial vitality of New Haven. Its style was innovative, providing for the first time in a large scale business building, wide shop windows, and three upper floors for a variety of organizations. Early occupants included Mouthrop's Museum and Apothecaries Hall, the city's first drugstore. Offices of the Mayor and administration were here prior to the construction of City Hall, as well as law offices including that of Roger Sherman Baldwin, defense attorney for the Amistad Captives.

Walk back diagonally across to the center of the lower Green past the World War I Memorial flagstaff (1928), designed by Douglas Orr toward Temple St.

The most beautiful and most photographed **view** in New Haven, the three churches on the Green were built over the period 1812-15. During the War of 1812 British blockade of New Haven, only ships carrying building materials for the churches were permitted entry to the harbor. View or visit the churches, from right *(north)* to left *(south)*.

United Congregational Church (North Church) – *323 Temple St. Visit by appointment only. ☎ 203-787-4195.* This Congregational church united two congregations that split off from the First Church in the aftermath of the Great Awakening in the mid-18C. The design, based originally on All Saints Church in Southampton, England and redrawn by several architects, resulted in this example of Federal architecture. Take note of the steeple, whose style has been replicated in churches throughout the country.

★ **Congregational United Church of Christ (Center Church)** – *250 Temple St. Visit by guided tour only Thur 11am–1pm. Crypt tours Sun morning after the 10 AM service and by appointment. ☎ 203-787-0121.* The formation of Center Church dates to 1639. Its original building was replaced in 1812 by this Georgian structure, now a National Historic Landmark. Architect Ithiel Town adapted a plan by Asher Benjamin of Boston that was based on the church of St. Martins-in-the-Field in London. As there was no heating system, large clear glass windows were placed to capture the maximum sunlight. The major decorative feature is a Tiffany window installed in 1890, depicting the first Sunday worship in New Haven led by the Rev. John Davenport. Under the church is the **crypt**, created when the structure was built over part of the old burial ground. Among the gravestones that may be viewed by visitors is that of Benedict Arnold's first wife, Margaret Mansfield. During the Amistad incident in the mid-19C, the congregation of this church was instrumental in gaining support for the Africans, who were being held in the New Haven jail. The composer Charles Ives was organist here while he was a Yale student.
Behind the church is the original burial ground. There have been no burials here since 1812. In the small fenced-in graveyard look for the monuments to Theophilus Eaton, the first governor of the New Haven Colony, and to John Dixwell, one of the regicides.

Trinity Church – *129 Church St. Open year-round Mon–Thu 10am–noon, Sat 9am–noon, Sun 7:45am–1pm. ☎ 203-624-3101.* The first Episcopal congregation in New Haven was founded in 1752. Designed by Ithiel Town, it is considered the first Gothic Revival church and probably the first Gothic Revival building constructed in the US. As an early example of Medieval architecture in America, Trinity Church was, at the time of its construction, more of a tourist attraction than its companion churches.

Cross Chapel St. Sharing the block with the Chapel Square Mall is the Yale Co-op.

 **Galileo's**

155 Temple St. ☎ 203-974-6859. For a quiet drink and great scenery, turn in to the Omni Hotel and take the elevator up 19 floors for a panoramic view of the city, Yale, and even the harbor.

Yale Co-op – 924 Chapel St. Founded by Yale students in 1885 as a campus bookstore, the Yale Co-op, now a downtown book and department store, was originally located in Connecticut Hall.

Turn right and proceed up Chapel St. to College St. Turn left.

Taft Apartments – *265 College St.* Completed in 1911, the Taft (formerly Taft Hotel) was the city's finest hotel for generations. US President William Howard Taft had an office suite there when he was a professor at Yale after his tenure as commander-in-chief. The Taft was home to stage stars performing at the Shubert next door and is remembered as the site for several scenes in the film classic *All About Eve.*

 **Union League Cafe**

1032 Chapel St. ☎ 203-562-4299. Treat yourself to a little bit of New Haven history and great cuisine at this French-inspired brasserie located just off the Green. Site of the home of New Haven's first mayor, Roger Sherman, who, by the way, also signed the Declaration of Independence, the Articles of Confederation and the Constitution, the graciously restored Sherman Building offers patrons a beautiful, elegant yet unpretentious and relaxed setting for enjoying old and new world delicacies.

Shubert Performing Arts Center – *247 College St. Box office open Mon–Sat 10am–5pm, Sun 11am–3pm. ☎ 203-624-1825.* Since the Shubert Theatre opened in 1914, thousands of productions have been held at "The Birthplace of the Nation's Greatest Hits." It earned its "birthplace" appellation by offering—during its first 60 years—more than 300 world premieres, some 50 American premieres, and about 200 shows prior to their debuts in New York. The totals are double that of any theater in New York or any other try-out cities like Boston, Philadelphia or Washington. In 1976 the Shubert closed, reopening in 1984 as the not-for-profit Shubert Performing Arts Center. During this time the Theater underwent a multi-million dollar renovation, restoring the original theater and adding a new glass-walled lobby front. Next door is the Shubert Square Theater Boutique.

Across College Street from the Taft is the **Owl Shop** *(268 College St.)*, one of the oldest downtown businesses (1934). Said to be one of the largest and most complete pipe and tobacco shops in the country, the Owl blends its own tobacco and ships all over the world.

ADDITIONAL SIGHTS

★Grove Street Cemetery *Map p 40*

Located at 227 Grove St., the cemetery is open daily until 4pm. ☎ 203-787-1443. A brochure with a detailed map of grave site numbers and cemetery tour is available at the manager's office inside the gate.

The Grove Street Cemetery is one of the most historic cemeteries in the US. Many notable men and women of local and national importance are buried or memorialized here including: Eli Whitney, Noah Webster, Charles Goodyear, and most recently Glenn Miller. Incorporated in 1797 as the New Haven Burying Ground, it was the first chartered cemetery in the US and the first to be laid out in lots for families and special groups. Before that time the city's burial ground was the area of the New Haven Green behind Center Church. After 250 years of use, the Green was crowded with perhaps as many as 5,000 graves, and a new cemetery was planned at the edge of the nine squares by a group of citizens led by Sen. James Hillhouse. Stones that had not been removed from the Green after twenty-five years were taken to the Grove Street Cemetery and are arranged alphabetically along the west side and rear walls. The striking Egyptian Revival **gateway★** was designed by Henry Austin in 1845. Inscribed across the top is the biblical quotation, "The Dead Shall be Raised." Since Yale buildings now surround the cemetery, the saying has prompted the rejoinder, "But not until Yale needs the land."

Listed below are a few highlights of the cemetery tour. At the gate, enter and turn left. Walk to Cedar Ave., the "Avenue of the Worthies," and turn right.

No. 7 – Benjamin Silliman (1779-1864), father of scientific education in America.

No. 12 – Lyman Beecher (1775-1863), abolitionist and father of Henry Ward Beecher and Harriet Beecher Stowe.

No. 13 – Eli Whitney (1765-1825), inventor of the cotton gin and the American system of manufacture.

No. 14 – Noah Webster (1758-1843), author of the first American dictionary.

No. 19 – Leonard Bacon (1802-81), abolitionist, benefactor of the Amistad Captives, and clergyman whose writings inspired Abraham Lincoln. Nearby is the grave of his sister Delia Bacon (1811-59), author and originator of the Baconian theory of the authorship of Shakespeare's plays.

Continue toward the rear of the cemetery to view the early headstones arranged against the back wall. Turn left, then left again to walk back on Sycamore Ave.

No. 27 – Charles Goodyear (1800-60), inventor of vulcanized rubber.

From Sycamore Ave. cross Spruce and Cedar Aves. Turn left onto Locust Ave.

At this corner is the Yale lot, around **Nos. 38** and **39**, where several students and professors are buried. Of special note is the new stone for **Mary Goodman** (d.1872), an African American New Havener who left her entire estate of about $5,000 to establish the first scholarship fund to educate African American men for the ministry at the Yale Divinity School.

Return down Locust Ave. to return to the gate.

Wooster Square

To drive from the Green to Wooster Square, from Temple St. turn left onto Chapel St. Continue down Chapel St. crossing Church, Orange, and State Sts. Proceed over the bridge and continue on Chapel crossing Union St. To park, continue down Chapel St. to Wooster Square. Two-hour parking is available weekdays 8am–7pm or anytime on weekends or evenings on Wooster Pl., Greene St., and Academy St. The walking tour begins at the intersection of Olive and Chapel Sts.

Four blocks east of the Green is a gracious and historic park, named for General David Wooster, a Revolutionary War hero. Featuring some of the most beautiful architecture in New Haven, this restored historic district offers benches beneath flowering cherry trees and a monument to Christopher Columbus, unveiled in 1892, on the 400th anniversary celebration of his voyage. In 1970 the area around Wooster Square was designated as New Haven's first historic district. Most of its historic residences are mid-Victorian in the Italian villa style, with some in the Greek Revival style.

The square was the center of an area of New Haven that began to grow rapidly with the opening of the Farmington Canal in 1825. When the railroad came to the city in 1839, business flourished as New Haven's manufactured goods could easily reach new markets. Large factories for the making of carriages, clocks, and hardware were built, as well as many smaller ones. As the factory owners prospered they wanted to build large houses in a fashionable area near their businesses. The most affluent homes were built in the Wooster Square neighborhood while the homes of skilled workers, managers, and tradesmen were built on the smaller streets nearby. At first most of the people who lived in the area were of Protestant English ancestry, but after 1880, new immigrants began to move in, mainly Italians and Jews. The Congregational Church facing the square built in 1855 has served as a Baptist Church, and in 1899 became St. Michael's Roman Catholic Church. By the early 20C, the Wooster Square neighborhood was predominantly Italian. A preservation movement was launched in the late 1950s and 1960s after the neighborhood was threatened with demolition in the early redevelopment era.

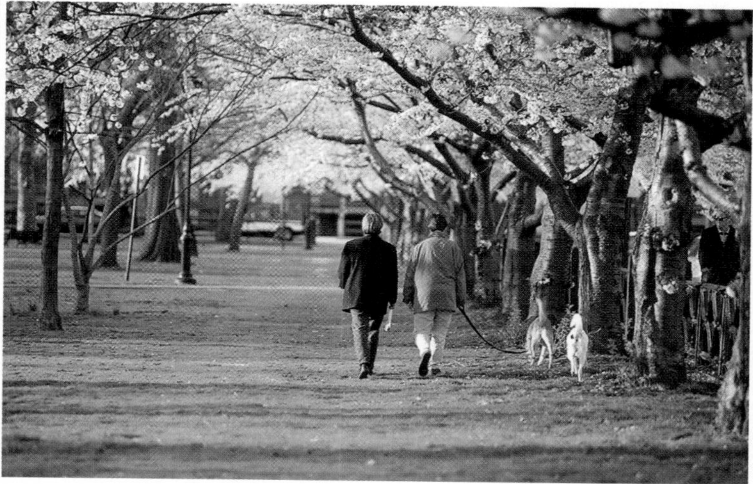

Michael Marsland /Yale University

Walking Tour

Beginning on the corner of Olive and Chapel Streets, **nos. 621, 613, 607, 604** are all Henry Austin designs. Not far from the Italianate **no. 600**, imposing **no. 584** is another Austin design constructed for Willis Bristol, a New Haven businessman and banker.

Cross to Wooster Square and from Chapel Street turn left onto Academy Street to **no. 20**, the last private house (1885) built on the square; from 1919-1940, it was the home and office of Michael Riccio, the Royal Consular Agent of Italy. At left is **Court Street** (1869-79) whose row houses were rehabilitated in 1961. At **no. 42**, the Edward Rowland House (1857), turn right crossing Academy Street to **311 Greene Street★**, the Max Adler House (1879). A Jewish immigrant from Germany in the 1840s, Adler started out as a tailor and worked his way up to the ownership of the largest corset factory business in the world. The old Strouse-Adler Corset factory, still standing a block away on Olive Street, closed in 1999.

Turn right into Wooster Square. Continue down the path to the center of the park. Turn left to Wooster Pl.

Upon exiting the park, turn right and continue down Wooster Place to **no. 9**, the mansard-roofed Stephen Jewett House (1833). Proceed to **no. 7**, the Russell Hotchkiss House (1844), whose romantic cast iron balconies added in the 1850s provide credence to the story that southern families, especially those from New Orleans, summered in the square.

■ Wooster Street Eating

From Academy St. turn right onto Chapel St. From Chapel turn left onto Olive St. then left onto Wooster St. When you mention Wooster Street to a New Havener be prepared for them to step out of their reserved, New England demeanor and launch into a passionate discussion about the city's famous pizza. Great pizza places abound throughout the city, but Sally's *(no. 237)* and Pepe's *(no. 157)* are the institutions. Frank Pepe served up his first pizza in 1900, and his brick ovens have been pleasing palates ever since. Cuisine of most of the restaurants on Wooster Street still reflects the neighborhood's Italian heritage, so after grabbing a slice or sitting down to some great seafood or pasta, stroll over to Libby's Italian Pastry Shop *(139 Wooster St. ☎ 203-772-0380)* for your daily requirement of *gelati* or *dolci*.

New Haven Colony Historical Society – *114 Whitney Ave. Open Sept–Jun Tue–Fri 10am–5pm, weekends 2pm–5pm. Rest of the year Tue–Fri 10am–5pm, Sat 2pm–5pm. Closed major holidays $2. ♿ 🅿 ☎ 203-562-4183.* Featuring local fine arts, decorative arts, and maritime history, the society also preserves notable artifacts including an original model and full-size working version of Eli Whitney's cotton gin, one of Samuel F.B. Morse's first code receivers, Charles Goodyear's rubber inkwell, and a reconstruction of the first telephone switchboard. The exhibit, "Cinque Lives Here" documents the Amistad Affair and includes the society's famous portrait of Cinque, the leader of the captives. The Whitney Library contains about 30,000 printed items and over 250 manuscript collections devoted to the region's history.

East Rock Park – *Follow Orange St. Cross Mill River and turn left, then bear right. The road leads to the summit parking lot. Open mid-Apr–Oct daily 8am–dusk. Rest of the year weekends & holidays only 8am–dusk. ☎ 203-946-6086.* New Haven's oldest park includes walking trails, a road to the summit, Soldiers and Sailors Monument, the Giant Steps up the cliff, a ranger station and playground at College Woods, a rose garden and athletic fields. From the summit of this basalt ridge there is a great **view★★** of the entire New Haven area. In the distance stretches Long Island Sound.

EXCURSIONS *See p 83 for a listing of New Haven area parks.*

Eli Whitney Museum – *915 Whitney Ave., Hamden. Open year-round Wed–Fri noon–5pm, Sat 10am–3pm, Sun noon–5pm. 🅿 ☎ 203-777-1833.* Exhibits "Inventing Change" and "The Gilbert Gallery," on scientific toy maker A.C. Gilbert, highlight the innovative techniques of New Haven inventors. From November to January the annual Toy Train exhibition allows visitors to run as many as four separate train lines on a 30ft x 15ft layout. Across the street from the museum is Eli Whitney's barn and the boarding house occupied by his workers, now the headquarters of the Connecticut Trust for Historical Preservation.

Farmington Canal Trail – *Begins at Todd St., Hamden.* ☎ *203-785-1482.* The original canal trail that ran 80 miles from New Haven to Massachusetts is being preserved for its historical significance and for recreational purposes. An 8.5mi stretch from Hamden Hills to Cornwall Street in Cheshire is now open for biking, jogging, hiking and rollerblading. Public parking is available at Todd Street, Sherman Avenue, or Brooksvale Park in Hamden.

Shoreline Trolley Museum – Kids *5mi east of New Haven, in East Haven, by I-95. 17 River St. Take Exit 51, turn right onto Hemingway Ave., then left onto River St. Open Memorial Day–Labor Day daily 11am–5pm. May, Sept, Oct & Dec weekends only 11am–5pm. Apr & Nov Sun only 11am–5pm. Closed Thanksgiving Day, Dec 25. $5. A 3mi trolley excursion takes riders along the Connecticut shore between the museum and Short Beach.* ♿ P ☎ *203-467-6927.* Volunteer trolley buffs have restored one-third of the nearly 100 street, subway and elevated railway cars on the grounds.

Sleeping Giant State Park – *6mi from New Haven. Take Whitney Ave. (Rte. 10) to Hamden and turn right on Mt. Carmel Ave. Open year-round daily 8am–dusk. Trail maps and information available at ranger headquarters.* ☎ *203-789-7498.* This park north of New Haven provides 33mi of hiking trails, picnicking and fishing on approximately 1,500 acres of land. **Tower Path** *(1.3mi each way)* leads to the highest point in the park, where, from a stone tower, there are great **views★★** of the region.

Baccalaureate, Woolsey Hall

Michael Marsland/Yale University

Practical Information

Planning Your Trip

Visitors can contact the following agencies to obtain maps and information on points of interest, accommodations and seasonal events:

Greater New Haven Convention and Visitors Bureau ☎ 203-777-8550 800-332-7829
59 Elm St.
New Haven, CT 06511
www.newhavencvb.org

Yale University Visitor Information Center ☎ 203-432-2300
149 Elm Street
P.O. Box 201942
New Haven, CT 06520-1942
www.yale.edu/visitor

New Haven's Seasons

New Haven's four distinct seasons each lend a particular character to the city. Most tourists visit during the mild months of April, May, September and October.

Spring – Beginning in late March and lasting through the end of May, spring daytime highs usually reach the low 60°sF (20°C) and nighttime lows rarely dip below 40°F (4°C). From late March though May, sunny days may give way to rain or to snow showers (not uncommon in April).

Summer – Generally mild, daytime temperatures along the coast average 70 to 80°F (21 to 27°C), with July being the warmest month. Summer nights tend to be cool and comfortable.

Autumn – Lasting from mid-September through October, autumn may be the most pleasant time to visit New Haven. Crisp, clear days with temperatures in the 50°sF and 60°sF (10-20°C) give way to cool nights, usually dropping into the 40°sF (4-8°C). Hints of the impending winter may appear with an occasional frost and freeze warning.

Winter – Daytime temperatures average between 20-40°F (–7°C to 4°C); nights drop to 15-20°F (–9°C to –7°C). Snowfall averages 25in a year. Protective clothing (coats, boots, gloves, hats) is essential when venturing outside.

New Haven Temperature Chart *(recorded at Tweed-New Haven Airport)*

	average high	average low	precipitation
January	36°F (2°C)	22°F (–5°C)	3.2in (8.1cm)
April	57°F (12°C)	40°F (4°C)	3.8in (9.7cm)
July	82°F (28°C)	66°F (19°C)	3.9in (9.9cm)
October	64°F (18°C)	50°F (10°C)	3.1in (7.9cm)

Getting to New Haven

By Air

New Haven is served by two major airports *(map p 90)*.

Tweed-New Haven Regional Airport (HVN) – *www.tweednewhavenairport.com ☎ 203-466-8833. 4.7mi east of Yale University Visitor Information Center.* US Airways Express arrives at and departs from Tweed-New Haven. Smoking is prohibited in the airport.

Taxis – Available at the side entrance to Tweed outside the baggage claim area, taxi service to downtown New Haven takes approximately 15min and costs on average $9-$11.

Shuttles – Many hotels offer shuttle service to and from Tweed. A call station is located in the baggage claim area.

Rental Cars – *p 81*. Avis, Hertz and Budget rental-car companies are located at the baggage claim area of the main terminal. At the airport, a sales tax of 9.18% plus an airport fee of 10% are added to the rental rate.

Public Transportation – CTTransit provides round-trip bus service to Tweed-New Haven airport from all areas of the city ☎ 203-624-0151.

Bradley International Airport (BDL) – *www.bradleyairport.com ☎ 860-292-2000. 52mi north of downtown New Haven, in Windsor Locks, CT.* International flights and domestic flights arrive at and depart from Bradley. **A Traveler's Aid Booth** *(open year-round daily 9am–7pm)* is located on the upper level of both terminals. Smoking is prohibited in the airport. **Restaurants** with sit-down service are located on the upper level of both terminals. **Public transportation** departs from the lower level of both terminals.

Taxis – Taxis are available from ground transportation service coordinators located near baggage claim areas from 7am–1am. Taxi service to downtown Hartford takes about 20min and costs on average $28. Airport Taxi Co. ☎ 1-888-235-8294; Yellow Cab Co. ☎ 860-666-6666.

Shuttles – **Connecticut Limousine** *www.ctlimo.com* ☎ 800-472-5466 provides shuttle service from Bradley International Airport to New Haven *($24 one way)*. Airport Connection ☎ 860-627-3400 provides shuttle service from Bradley to Union Station, Hartford *($11 one way)*. Peter Pan bus service ☎ 800-237-8747 provides continuing service from Union Station, Hartford to New Haven *($11 one way/$20 round-trip)*.

Rental Cars – *p 81*. Rental-car company courtesy telephones are located in baggage claim areas of both terminals. Shuttles pick up passengers at the outer curb of the lower level. At the airport, a sales tax of 6%, a $1 CT Tourism surcharge and a 3% CT surcharge tax are added to the rental rate; some car companies add a daily surcharge.

Public Transportation – CTTransit provides transportation between the Old State House in Hartford and Bradley International Airport.

By Shuttle from New York City Airports

Connecticut Limousine *(☎ 203-878-2222; 800-472-5466)* offers service to JFK and La Guardia airports *($38 one way/$72 round-trip)*. Buses make frequent stops and trips can take up to 2 1/2 hrs. Trips to Newark can last up to 3 hrs *($41 one way/$78 round-trip)*. **Prime Time** *(☎ 800-733-8267)* offers door-to-door service to JFK and La Guardia *($43 one way)* from New Haven hotels. **Red Dot Limousine** *(☎ 800-673-3368)* services JFK and La Guardia *($43/one way)*.

By Train

Union Station is New Haven's only railroad station and offers **Amtrak**, **Metro-North**, and **Shoreline East** rail service. Located across from the New Haven Police Department on Union Ave., the station is accessible by CTTransit (routes A, U, & J). **Metro-North** *www.mta.nyc.ny.us* offers daily service between New Haven and New York ☎ 212-532-4900. **Amtrak** provides direct daily service between New Haven and major destinations throughout the Northeast (from New Haven to New York, Boston and Washington, DC via Philadelphia and New York). Beginning in 2000 Amtrak's high speed service comes to the northeast corridor. Advance reservations are recommended to ensure the best fares and desired accommodations. Major short-distance routes to New Haven are from Philadelphia *(3 1/2 hrs)*, New York *(1 1/2 hrs)* and Boston (3 hrs). Amtrak also offers daily service between Hartford and New Haven. Travelers from Canada should ask their local travel agents about Amtrak/VIARail connections. The **Explore America Pass** allows up to 45 days of travel nationwide (limited to three stops). The **USA RailPass** (not available to US or Canadian citizens or legal residents) offers unlimited travel within Amtrak-designated regions at discounted rates: 15- and 30-day passes are available. For schedules and routes, visit Amtrak's website at www.amtrak.com or call ☎ 800-872-7245 *(toll-free in North American only; outside North America, contact your local travel agent)*. **Shore Line East** *www.rideworks.com* provides commuter rail service Mon–Fri from Union Station between New Haven and Branford, Guilford, Madison, Clinton, Westbrook, Old Saybrook, and New London ☎ 203-777-7433.

By Bus

Greyhound provides access to New Haven at fares that are generally lower than air or rail rates. However, some travelers may find long-distance bus travel uncomfortable due to the lack of sleeping accommodations. The **Ameripass** allows unlimited travel for 7, 15, 30 or 60 days. Advance reservations are suggested. For fares, schedules and routes, call ☎ 800-231-2222. The city's main bus terminal is located at Union Station on Union Ave. across from the New Haven Police Dept. **Peter Pan** offers service throughout the Northeastern portion of the US. Schedule and route information: ☎ 800-343-9999.

By Car

Map p 90. New Haven is situated at the crossroads of interstate routes: I-95 (east-west) and I-91 (north-south).

Admission prices and hours published in this guide are accurate at press time.

Getting Around New Haven

A Downtown for Walkers

The principal sights and university buildings, and entertainment and business centers are concentrated in and around the New Haven Green. The city's most heavily visited areas, such as the Chapel Street shops, Shubert Performing Arts Center, and university museums and libraries, where parking is limited, are best visited on foot. During **rush hours**—the peak transit times for business commuters *(7am–9:30am and 4pm–6:30pm)*, visitors should be aware of fast-moving vehicles in traffic lanes close to the sidewalks. Compliance with pedestrian walking signs is expected.

Public Transportation

Connecticut Transit *(☎ 203-624-0151)* operates a public bus system that links New Haven and the surrounding areas. Buses generally operate Monday–Friday 5:30am–1am, Saturday 6am–1am, Sunday and holidays 7am–midnight. Bus stops are indicated by red and white signs. The buses display the route number and final destination above the windshield. **Fares** are $1/person. Exact fare is required. Bus-to-bus transfers are free. Ask driver for transfer ticket when boarding bus. All buses are accessible to riders with disabilities. The CTTRANSIT Information Center is located on Chapel Street at the New Haven Green. To request a schedule, call ☎ 203-624-0151 or consult its website www.cttransit.com.

Taxis

Within the city of New Haven, it is difficult to hail a taxi on the street. Call the dispatcher at least 1 hr in advance. Rates for taxis are $1.60 per person then $.20 for each 1/7 mile and $.20 per minute of waiting time. Taxis should follow the meters and not charge fixed rates.

Taxi services in the New Haven area include

	☎
Metro Taxi	203-777-7777
New Haven	203-877-0000
Yellow Cab	203-777-5555
Valley Cab	203-924-8294
Milford Taxi & Courier Co., Inc.	203-877-1468
Orange Taxi Cab Co.	203-877-1460
Fairfield Cab Co.	203-255-5797

Driving in New Haven

Given the proximity of major Yale and New Haven sights, it is highly recommended that you stay in downtown New Haven and visit the city and university on foot. However, it is probably best to use a car or taxi if visiting Wooster Square or its restaurants in the evening. The area's parks and surrounding attractions make car travel a necessity. Keep in mind that street parking is limited. If you are driving to New Haven from the surrounding areas, it is recommended that you take advantage of all day parking garages located around downtown.

Road Regulations – The maximum **speed limit** on major expressways is 65mph in rural areas and 55mph in and around cities. The speed limit within the city is 25mph unless otherwise posted. The use of **seat belts** is mandatory for driver and passengers. Child safety seats are required for children under four years or weighing less than 40 pounds (seats available from most rental-car agencies). Drivers must always yield the **right of way** to pedestrians. Connecticut school bus law requires motorists to bring vehicles to a full stop when warning signals on a school bus are flashing. Unless otherwise posted, drivers may turn right on a red traffic light after coming to a complete stop.

Parking – In the city, parking space on the street is limited and parking regulations are strictly enforced. Some metered parking is available. Yale lots are open to the public free of charge on evenings and weekends. Parking in some residential areas is by permit only (restricted to area residents). In the Wooster Square area, nonresidents are allowed to park for a maximum of two hours between 8am and 7pm; after 7pm, parking is unregulated unless otherwise posted. Parking spaces reserved for specific use by permit only are reserved 24 hrs daily unless otherwise specified. Parking spaces identified with ♿ are reserved for people with disabilities; anyone parking in these spaces without a valid state permit is subject to a heavy fine. Private parking garages are easy to find throughout the central sections of the city.

Car Rentals – Major rental-car agencies have offices downtown and at the airports *(p 78)* serving the metropolitan area. Some agencies will rent only to persons at least 25 years old; others rent to drivers age 21 to 24 years for a daily surcharge. A major credit card and a valid driver's license are required for rental (some agencies also require proof of insurance). The daily rate for a compact car when renting for 5–7 days ranges from $32 to $44. Note that car rentals are taxed 12% in CT.

Rental Company	☎ Reservations
Acme Rent-A-Car	203-865-2105
Alamo	800-327-9633
Avis	800-331-1212
Budget	800-527-0700
Enterprise	800-736-8222
Hertz	800-654-3131
National	800-227-7368
Rent A Wreck	800-535-1391
Sears Car & Truck Rental	800-527-0770
Thrifty	800-367-2277

(Toll-free numbers may not be accessible outside North America.)

Basic Information

Mail – Post Office at 206 Elm Street is open Monday to Friday 8am–5pm and Saturday 8am–noon. For location and hours of local post offices and other information, contact the Postal Service Customer Call Center *(Mon–Fri 8am–6pm, Sat 7:30am–4pm)* ☎ 800-275-8777.

First-class rates within the US: letter 33¢ (1oz), postcard 20¢. Overseas: letter 60¢ (1/2oz), postcard 50¢. Letters can be mailed from most hotels. Stamps and packing material may be purchased at post offices, grocery stores and businesses offering postal and express shipping services located throughout the city *(see Yellow Pages of the phone directory under "Mailing Services" or "Post Offices")*.

Newspapers and Magazines – The city's leading daily, the *New Haven Register*, provides mostly local news with limited national and international coverage. The weekend section in the Friday edition lists entertainment, special events, and attractions for children. The Sunday edition contains a section highlighting the arts. The *New Haven Advocate*, a free weekly newspaper, features listings of restaurants, upcoming events and stories about the city and is available in boxes on downtown and area streets. The *Yale Bulletin & Calendar* covers university news and the local entertainment scene. The *Greater New Haven Visitor's Guide Book* (found at hotels) features practical information and listings of cultural events, restaurants, nightspots and shops.

Safety Tips

When visiting New Haven, you are encouraged to use the same care in safeguarding your possessions that you observe elsewhere:

- Keep your hotel room locked, and leave valuables at home if you do not need them during your travels.
- Lock your car and store any items in the trunk or out of sight.
- In case you need assistance or have an emergency on the Yale campus, blue telephones illuminated by a blue light provide a direct connection to the Yale Police.
- New Haven Police are available by dialing 911 from telephones off campus.
- Hospitality officers serve the downtown area including the Green; they can answer questions, offer directions, and provide other assistance.

Taxes and Tipping – In New Haven the general sales tax is 6%. The hotel tax is 12%; rental-car tax is 12%; and the food and beverage tax (restaurants) is 6%. Sales taxes in neighboring areas outside New Haven vary depending on the city.

In restaurants it is customary to tip the server 15-20% of the bill. Taxi drivers usually receive 15% of the fare. Skycabs and porters are generally tipped $1 per bag and hotel maids $1 per night.

Telephone – A local call generally costs 25¢ from a pay phone.

Important Numbers

Emergency Police/Ambulance/Fire Department (24hrs) **911**

Police *(non-emergency)* 203-946-6316

Yale-New Haven Hospital *(emergency)* 203-688-2222

(non-emergency) 203-688-4242

Pharmacies:

Rite Aid, 900 Chapel Square Mall 203-777-7248

CVS, 1168 Whalley Ave. 203-387-6784

Poison Control Center *(24hrs)* 800-343-2722

Time 203-777-4647

Weather .... 888-254-5584 ext. 3030

Television and Radio

Major TV Networks		
ABC......Channel 8	CBS......Channel 3	PBS......Channel 65
NBC......Channel 30	FOX .....Channel 5	CNN .....*cable channel varies*

Major FM Radio Stations		Major AM Radio Stations
NPR............91.1	Classical............91.5	CNNnews 1360AM
Country.......92.5	Jazz/talk...........89.5	News/sports 1410AM
Rock...........99.1	Contemporary...99.9	Oldies..........102.9

Time Zone – New Haven is located in the Eastern Standard Time (EST) zone, which is five hours behind Greenwich Mean Time. Daylight Saving Time is observed from the first Sunday in April (clocks are advanced 1hr) to the last Sunday in October.

Sightseeing

Yale University Walking Tour – *149 Elm St. ☎ 203-432-2300.* Student-led tours leave from the Yale Visitor Information Center Mon–Fri 10:30am & 2pm, weekends 1:30pm.

New Haven First Walking Tour – *April–Oct Thu at noon. Leaves from Yale Visitor Information Center, 149 Elm St. ☎ 203-432-2302 or 203-777-8550.* This guided general interest tour of downtown New Haven is sponsored by various city, civic, arts and historical groups. The one-hour tour covers the downtown area around the historic New Haven Green.

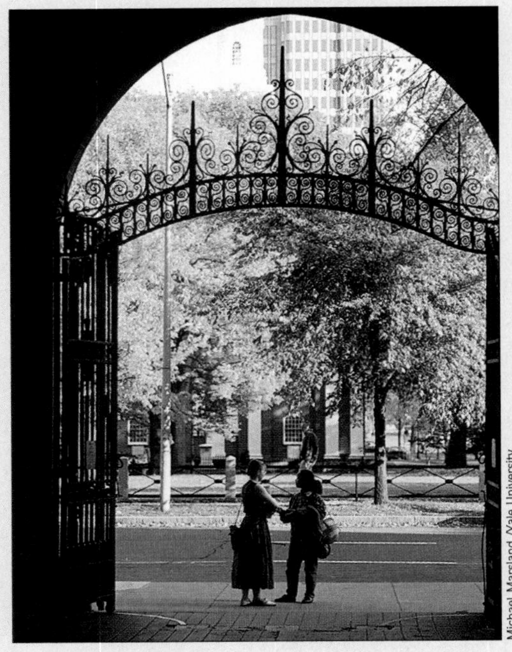

Michael Marsland /Yale University

Recreation

New Haven has designated 17 percent of the city's 21.2 sq mi area for parks. Add to this area state parks, and there is plenty of room for recreational activities. For more information contact the **New Haven Dept. of Parks, Recreation & Trees** ☎ 203-946-8025. Step outdoors to enjoy the fall foliage or take a summertime cruise around Long Island Sound or to the nearby Thimble Islands.

Parks

East Rock Park – *Description p 74.*

East Shore Park – *Woodward Ave. (I-95, exit 50). ☎ 203-946-8790.* Located along New Haven Harbor, this park has something for everyone with its walking, jogging and inline skating trails; softball, baseball and soccer fields, tennis and basketball courts.

Edgerton Park – *Whitney Ave. at Cliff St.* The design of this peaceful 22-acre park listed on the National Register of Historic Places was based on an 18C English landscape garden. With facilities for walking and biking, the park features a tropical greenhouse, community garden center and horticulture library open on Sunday afternoons.

Edgewood Park – *Edgewood Ave. between Whalley Ave. and Chapel St. ☎ 203-946-8028.* Edgewood Park features the Holocaust memorial, Spanish American War monument, nature walks and a duck pond, tennis and basketball courts, soccer and Little League fields. Near the playground, the ranger station houses wildlife displays.

Fort Nathan Hale & Black Rock Fort – *End of Woodward Ave. (I-95, exit 50). Open Memorial Day–Labor Day daily 10am–5pm; autumn weekends 10am–5pm. ☎ 203-946-8790.* Historic displays at Black Rock Fort (Revolutionary War) and Fort Nathan Hale (Civil War) have been restored and are open to visitors.

Greenbrier Greenhouse & Crosby Conservatory – *75 Cliff St. Open Mar–Oct Mon–Fri 10am–5pm, weekends 10am–4pm. Nov–Feb daily 10am–4pm ☎ 203-777-1886.* A vocational program run by Easter Seals maintains this greenhouse and conservatory located in Edgerton Park. The greenhouse sells seasonal plants year-round, features a children's corner for young horticulturists, and sponsors activities for New Haven schoolchildren. The conservatory, maintained by the Greenbrier program, holds a collection of tropical plants with a rainforest corner.

Lighthouse Point Park, Carousel & Beach – *End of Townsend Ave. (I-95, exit 50). Open year-round daily. ☎ 203-946-8790.* Lighthouse Park has a public beach for swimming and picnicking, a restored antique carousel *(seasonal)*; playing fields and nature recreation.

Long Wharf Nature Preserve – *I-95, exit 46.* Walkers can enjoy the seaside wildlife on this trail along Long Island Sound.

Milford Point Sanctuary – *1 Milford Point Road, Milford, CT. ☎ 203-878-7440.* Connecticut Audubon Coastal Center is a sanctuary for birds. Lecture series, bird walks, family programs and craft workshops are available.

Pardee Rose Garden – *180 Park Rd., Hamden. Open mid-May–early Sept. ☎ 203-946-8142.* Picnic areas are available in this tranquil formal rose garden open free to the public. The garden is also available for weddings and special events for a small permit fee.

Quinnipiac River Park – *Front St. between Grand Ave. and Chapel St.* The restoration of this lovely riverside park was completed in 1992. Relax on a bench or walk along the river while you watch the turnbridge on Grand Avenue accommodate local small craft traveling the river.

Regional Water Authority Hiking – *90 Sargent Dr. (I-95, exit 46). ☎ 203-624-6671.* Over 50 miles of wide, marked trails are open to the public for hiking, jogging and bird watching throughout West Haven, Orange, Woodbridge and the shoreline towns east of New Haven.

Sleeping Giant State Park – *Description p 75.*

Vietnam Veterans Memorial Park – *On the Waterfront (I-95, exit 46).* Seventeen acres lining the west shore of New Harbor offer walkways, benches and public parking.

Vision Legacy Trail – *Harbor waterfront (I-95, exit 46) at Canal Dock Rd.; New Haven Green at Chapel St. ☎ 203-782-4310.* This commemorative brick walkway, connecting downtown New Haven with the harbor and West Haven's Savin Rock, is part of the East Coast Greenway. When completed, the Greenway will be an 80 % off-road, non-motorized route from Maine to Florida.

West River Park – *Ella T. Grasso Blvd. between Rte. 1 and Rte. 34.* Adjacent to Edgewood Park, West River Park features public soccer and softball fields.

West Rock Nature Center – *Whalley Ave. to Fitch St. to Wintergreen Ave. (Merritt Pkwy., exit 61). Open year-round Mon–Fri 10am–4pm, Sat 11am–3pm. ☎ 203-946-8016.* Staffed year-round by park rangers, the Nature Center's 40 acres feature native wildlife, trails, picnic areas, a nature house and, during the summer, a small organic garden and farm.

West Rock Ridge State Park – *Whalley Ave. to Fitch St. to Wintergreen Ave. (Merritt Pkwy., exit 61). Open year-round daily 8am–dusk. ☎ 203-789-7498.* This landmark Connecticut state park features Lake Wintergreen, Judges' Cave, and walking trails.

West Haven Beach – *Capt. Thomas Blvd. and Ocean Ave., West Haven, CT.* Enjoy approximately 3 miles of beach that overlooks the New Haven Harbor and Long Island Sound. The area features a boardwalk along the former Savin Rock amusement park, a popular area for kite-flying and walking, and well-groomed public beaches.

Alling Memorial Golf Course – *35 Eastern St. ☎ 203-946-8014.* New Haven's municipal golf course is open seasonally. The facility offers a clubhouse, pro shop, restaurant, golf carts, and senior citizen discounts. This city-owned golf course is professionally managed by New England Golf Corporation.

Cruises

Thimble Island Cruises – *Sea Mist Thimble Islands Cruise sightseeing tours on weekends from May 1–May 31, Jun 1–Labor Day Wed–Mon, weekends Sept–Oct. Tours depart from Stony Creek (I-95, exit 56).*

Islander	Sea Mist II	Volsunga III
☎ 203-397-3921	☎ *203-488-8905*	☎ *203-488-9978*

Schooner, Inc. – *60 South Water St. Operates Memorial Day–Labor Day. Educational Sea Adventure: Wed 6pm–9pm; Fri 6pm–9pm; Sun 1pm–4pm. Sunset Cruise: Sun 5pm-8 pm. http://pages.cthome.net/schooner ☎ 203-865-1737.* Explore the biology and maritime history of Long Island Sound on board the 91ft schooner, *Quinnipiack*, or view picturesque skylines on a sunset cruise.

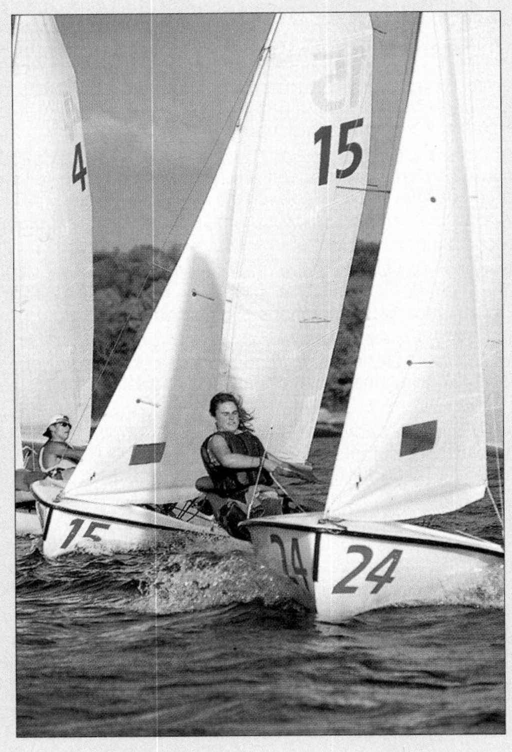

Michael Marsland /Yale University.

Shopping

The visitor to New Haven can find everything from specialty shops and boutiques on **Chapel** and **College Streets** to a variety of stores at the Chapel Square Mall.

Galleries, antique shops and bookstores can be found in the **Audubon Arts District** and around **Upper State Street.**

NEW HAVEN SHOPPING CENTER	*Address*	☎
Chapel Square Mall / *900 Chapel St.*		203-777-6661
(Small center with the Yale Co-Op and 38 specialty shops and eateries)		

OUTLYING SHOPPING MALL		☎
Milford		
Connecticut Post Mall	*1201 Boston Post Rd.*	203-878-6837

NEW HAVEN BOOKSTORES		☎
Afristar	*850 Grand Ave.*	203-772-7827
Arethusa Book Shop	*87 Audubon St.*	203-624-1848
Atticus Book Store-Café	*1082 Chapel St.*	203-776-4040
Blackprint Heritage Gallery	*162 Edgewood Ave.*	203-782-2159
Book Haven	*290 York St.*	203-787-2848
The Foundry Bookstore, Inc.	*33 Whitney Ave.*	203-624-8282
The Yale Book Store	*77 Broadway*	203-777-8440
Yale Co-Op	*924 Chapel St.*	203-772-2200
Bethany		
Whitlock Farm Booksellers	*20 Sperry Rd.*	203-393-1240

COLLEGIATE AND SPORTS PARAPHANALIA		☎
New Haven Ravens Dugout Store	*Yale Field 252 Derby Ave.*	203-782-1666
The Yale Bookstore	*77 Broadway*	203-777-8440
Yale Co-op	*924 Chapel St.*	203-772-2200
M & M Sports	*846 Chapel St.*	203-785-0045

FLEA MARKET		
Boulevard Flea Market	*510 Ella T. Grasso Blvd., Rte. 10*	203-772-1447

THEATER SHOP		
Shubert Square Theater Boutique	*247 College St.*	203-492-3891

MUSEUM SHOPS AND GALLERIES ☎

Below is a selection of New Haven galleries and university museums that maintain noteworthy shops on their premises:

Creative Arts Workshop	*80 Audubon St.*	203-562-2329
Gallery Raffael	*1177 Chapel St.*	203-772-2258
Peabody Museum of Natural History	*170 Whitney Ave.*	203-432-3740
The Wave Gallery	*1046 Chapel St.*	203-782-6212
Yale Center for British Art	*44 High St.*	203-432-2828
Yale University Art Gallery	*1111 Chapel St.*	203-432-0601

Spectator Sports

Yale offers 33 collegiate varsity sports *(www.yale.edu/athletic)* for men and women; the most popular for spectators are listed below. Tickets can be purchased at the venue or at the Ray Tompkins House *(20 Tower Pkwy)*, next to Payne Whitney Gymnasium. Call ☎ 203-432-YALE for up-to-date schedules, scores and information on Yale's varsity sports or ☎ 203-432-1400 for ticket orders.

Yale Sports

Sport	Season	Venue
Baseball	Mar–May	**Yale Field** 252 Derby Ave.
Basketball	Nov–Mar	**John J. Lee Amphitheater** **Payne Whitney Gymnasium** 70 Tower Pkwy.
Crew	Sept–Nov, Mar–Jun	**Gilder Boathouse** Rte. 34, Derby, CT
Football	Sept–Nov	**Yale Bowl** Derby Ave.
Hockey	Oct–Mar	**David S. Ingalls Rink** Prospect & Sachem Sts.
Lacrosse	Mar–May	**Soccer-Lacrosse stadium** Derby & Central Aves.
Soccer	Sept–Nov	**Soccer-Lacrosse stadium** Derby & Central Aves.
Softball	Mar–May	**Softball complex** Derby & Central Aves.
Tennis	Sept–May	**Cullman Courts** Derby Ave., across from Yale Field

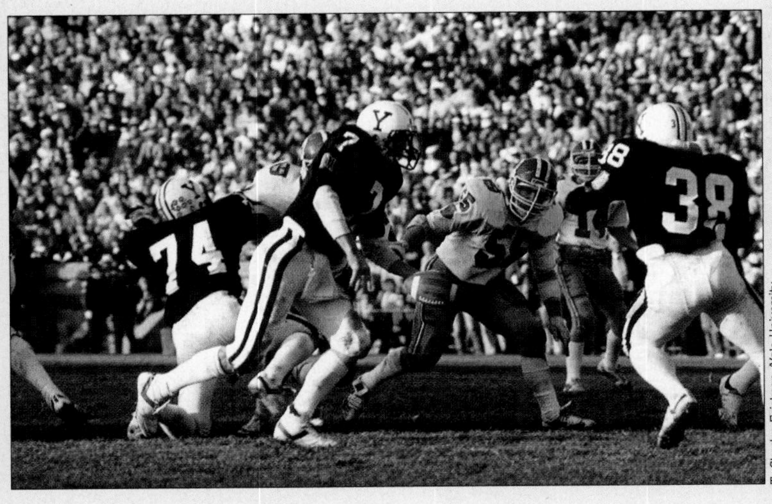
T. Charles Erickson /Yale University

Professional Sports

Tickets can usually be purchased at the venue. When games are sold out, you can sometimes get tickets through a ticket agency *(see the Yellow Pages of the phone directory)*.

Baseball	Season	Venue	☎
New Haven Ravens	**Apr–Sept**	**Yale Field** 252 Derby Ave.	203-782-1666 800-728-3671 *www.ravens.com*
Tennis			
Pilot Pen Women's International Tennis Tournament	**Aug**	**CT Tennis Center** 45 Yale Ave.	203-776-7331 888-997-4568 *www.pilotpentennis.com*

Performing Arts

New Haven provides visitors with a great diversity of performing arts offerings year-round. During the main concert season *(Sept–May)*, highly-respected dance, instrumental, choral and operatic performances are held primarily at the Shubert Performing Arts Center and at Yale's Woolsey Hall. The New Haven Symphony, the nation's fourth-oldest orchestra, has its own concert series and sponsors one featuring internationally known guest artists. Several live-performance theaters mount a variety of stage productions by traveling Broadway companies and acclaimed regional local groups; Yale University's Yale Repertory Theatre and New Haven's Long Wharf Theatre have both won regional theater Tony® awards. Popular rock and alternative music can be found at intimate and large-scale nightclubs as well as at stadiums and other large venues throughout New Haven. The Yale Bookstore and other bookstores and coffeehouses host public readings or talks by both established and up-and-coming authors.

Michael Marsland /Yale University

From June to August, Yale and New Haven host two major festivals: the 16 day **International Festival of Arts and Ideas**, which brings local and world-renowned artists, musicians and thinkers to city-wide venues, and the **New Haven Jazz Festival**, which brings internationally-renowned musicians to the city's Green for free, open-air concerts. The Yale School of Music summers in Norfolk, CT, and performs at the Norfolk Chamber Music Festival. *For a detailed listing of events, consult the New Haven Register* or the *New Haven Advocate, or the free publications listed* *on p 81*. Call ☎ 203-432-9100 for information on free Yale-sponsored performances.

Below is a selection of the area's performing arts organizations and venues:

Music

Yale University	Web site	☎	
Chamber Music Society	*www.yale.edu/schmus*	203-432-4157 203-432-4158	(recording) (box office)
Duke Ellington Fellowship Series	*www.yale.edu/schmus/ DE/index.htm*	203-432-4157 203-432-4158	(recording) (box office)
Great Organ Music at Yale	*www.yale.edu/schmus*	203-432-4157 203-432-4158	(recording) (box office)
New Music New Haven	*www.yale.edu/schmus/ orgs/orgsframes.html*	203-432-4157 203-432-4158	(recording) (box office)
Norfolk Chamber Music Festival	*www.yale.edu/norfolk*	860-542-3000	
Philharmonia Orchestra of Yale	*www.yale.edu/schmus/ orgs/orgsframes.html*	203-432-4157 203-432-4158	(recording) (box office)
Yale Bands: Concert Band, Jazz Ensemble	*www.yale.edu/yaleband*	203-432-4111	
Yale Camerata		203-432-5180	
Yale Collegium Musicum		203-432-2985	
Yale Glee Club	*www.yale.edu/ygc*	203-432-4136	
Yale Faculty Artist Series	*www.yale.edu/schmus*	203-432-4157 203-432-4158	(recording) (box office)
Yale Opera	*www.yale.edu/schmus/ orgs/orgsframes.html*	203-432-4157 203-432-4158	(recording) (box office)
Yale Symphony Orchestra	*www.yale.edu/yso*	203-432-4140	

New Haven	Web site	☎
Connecticut Chamber Orchestra		203-387-1376
International Festival of Arts and Ideas	*www.artidea.org*	(888)ART-IDEA
John Lyman Center for the Performing Arts, Southern Connecticut State University	*http://scsu.ctstateu.edu/~lyman_.htm*	203-392-6154
New Haven Chorale		203-787-1887
New Haven Jazz Festival		203-946-7173
New Haven Symphony Orchestra	*http://newhavensymphony.com*	203-776-1444
Orchestra New England	*www.orchestranewengland.org*	203-934-8863

Theater

Theaters and Companies	Address/Web site	☎
Algonkuin Theater Company		203-782-3675
Alliance Theater (University of New Haven)	300 Orange Ave., West Haven	203-230-2746
Amarante's Dinner Theater	62 Cove St.	203-467-2531
Crescent Players (Southern Connecticut State University)	501 Crescent St. *http://scsu.ctstateu.edu/~lyman_www/CP.htm*	203-392-6154
Long Wharf Theatre	222 Sargent Dr. *www.longwharf.org*	203-787-4282
New England Actors' Theater	150 Little Meadow Rd., Guilford *www.neatct.org*	203-458-7671
Yale Cabaret	217 Park St. *www.yale.edu/cabaret*	203-432-1566
Yale Dramatic Association (The Dramat)	222 York St. *www.yale.edu/dramat*	203-432-1212
Yale Repertory Theatre	1120 Chapel St. *www.yale.edu/yalerep*	203-432-1234
Shubert Performing Arts Center	247 College St. *www.shubert.com*	203-562-5666

Venues	Address	☎
Dodds Hall, University of New Haven	300 Orange Ave., West Haven	203-932-7085
John Lyman Center for the Performing Arts, Southern Connecticut State University	501 Crescent St.	203-392-6154
Little Theater of Lincoln Street, Educational Center for the Arts	Lincoln St. adjacent to Audubon Ct.	203-777-5451
New Haven Veterans Memorial Coliseum	275 So. Orange St.	203-772-4200 (ext. 212)
Palace Performing Arts Center	246 College St.	203-789-2120
Shubert Performing Arts Center	247 College St.	203-562-5666
Sprague Memorial Hall, Yale University	470 College St.	203-432-4157 (recording)
Woolsey Hall, Yale University	College & Grove Sts.	203-432-2310
Yale University Theatre	222 York St.	203-432-1234

FURTHER AFIELD

Only an hour or two away from New Haven lie great opportunities for adventure. Experience a little bit of literary history in Connecticut's capital, Hartford, where Mark Twain penned some of his most famous works, or pretend you are the captain of the fastest schooner on the seas at the beautiful and historic Mystic Seaport. Not far from the Seaport you can admire the diversity of the seas at Mystic Aquarium, then move on to the Mashantucket Pequot Museum to learn about life in a 16C Pequot Village.

HARTFORD★★

Population 139,739
Tourist Office ☎ 860-527-9258

Rising beside the Connecticut River, this Yankee city and state capital has been nicknamed "the Insurance Capital of the Nation," since the headquarters of so many insurance companies are located here.

★**Old State House** – *800 Main St. Open year-round Mon–Fri 10am–4pm, Sat 11am–4pm. Closed major holidays.* ♿ *☎ 860-522-6766.* Stop at the visitor center in this elegant Federal-style building (1792) for brochures and maps of Hartford. Legislative chambers contain original furnishings and the tiny museum displays taxidermic animals.

Travelers Tower Observation Deck – *1 Tower Square.* From this deck there is a very nice **view**★★ of the Hartford region *(visit by 30min guided tour only, mid-May–mid-Oct Mon–Fri 10am–3pm; closed major holidays; advance 1-day reservation suggested; 100 steps to climb; ☎ 860-277-4208; www.travelers.com).*

Max Downtown

CityPlace. ☎ 860-522-2530. Ask local residents and Max is usually mentioned top-of-mind as a favorite place to dine. Its American and Continental menu of beef, veal, fish and fowl offerings, served in an upscale milieu, is sure to please. The "GarBar," a cigar room, has been established for clientele who enjoy a puff. *Reservations advised.*

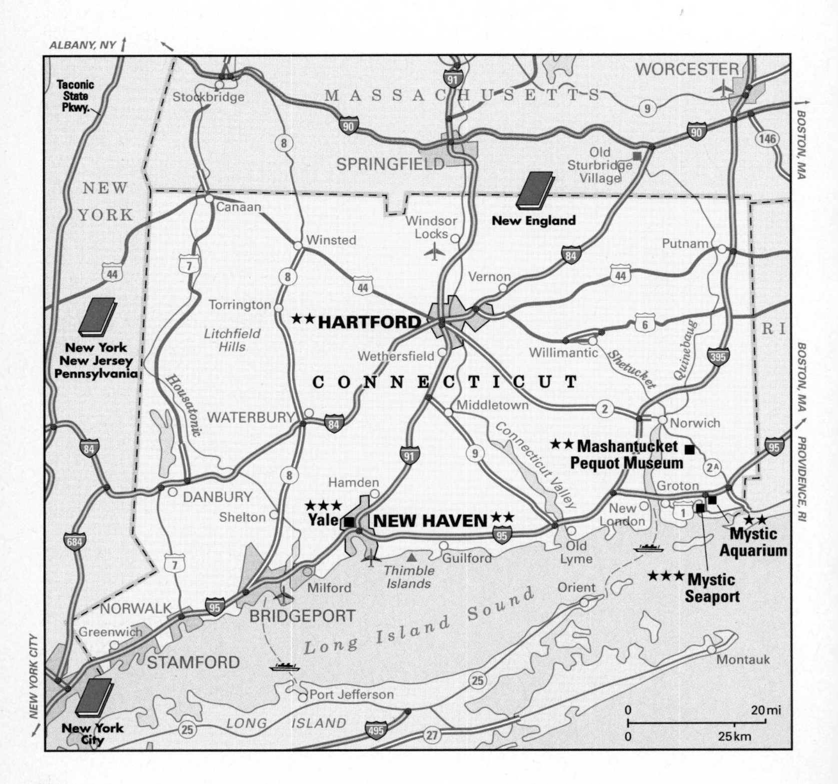

★★**Wadsworth Atheneum** – *600 Main St. Open year-round Tue–Sun 11am–5pm. Closed Jan 1, Jul 4, Thanksgiving Day, Dec 25. $7. ✗ ♿ ☎ 860-278-2670. www.wadsworthatheneum.org.* Founded in 1842, this formidable museum now houses 50,000 works spanning more than 5,000 years. Highlights include **European paintings** by Picasso, Mondrian and Dali as well as **sculpture** by Giacometti, Calder and David Smith, among others. **Morgan Great Hall** and adjacent galleries showcase Asian, Greek, Roman and Egyptian antiquities, European Medieval and Renaissance works and 17-19C European and American painting and sculpture. Amistad artifacts, African-American art from the 18C to 20C, prominent 17C and 18C European works by Caravaggio, Van Dyck, and Goya, decorative arts and a fine representation of American decorative arts round out the collection.

Modern Pastry Shop, Inc.

422 Franklin Ave. ☎ 860-296-7628. It's worth the drive to South Hartford to the Italian neighborhood located along Franklin Avenue, where there's a wide choice of dining establishments. But if time is short, stop at this bakery for cannoli and espresso. Try a custard accented with either chocolate or vanilla or the traditional ricotta cheese-filled cannoli. If you're still hungry, an assortment of cookies (almond paste, butter and chocolate), cakes, tortes, pies and over 30 Italian and French pastries awaits you.

★★**Mark Twain House** – *351 Farmington Ave. Take I-84 west to Exit 46. Turn right on Sisson Ave., then right on Farmington. Visit by guided tour (1hr) only, Memorial Day–mid-Oct & Dec Mon–Sat 9:30am–5pm, Sun 11am–5pm. Rest of the year Mon, Wed–Sat 9:30am–5pm, Sun noon–5pm. Closed major holidays. $9. P ☎ 860-493-6411. www.hartnet.org/twain.* A restoration of this historic home's 1881 decoration reveals silver stenciling, elaborately carved woodwork, and exquisite wall coverings. Twain slept backward in his bed in order to face its carved headboard and did most of his best writing in the Billiard Room.

MYSTIC SEAPORT★★★

The village of **Mystic**, on the Mystic River, has been a shipbuilding center since the 17C. Today Mystic is known primarily as the site of Mystic Seaport, a museum-village that re-creates the atmosphere of America's maritime past.

VISIT *1 day*

Kids *From I-95 Exit 90, follow Rte. 27 south. Open Apr–Oct daily 9am–5pm. Rest of the year daily 10am–4pm. Closed Dec 25. $16. Schedule of daily events and map are available at entrance. ✗ ☎ 860-572-5315. www.mysticseaport.org. Begin at the visitor center (main entrance), where a video offers a good introduction.*

The 1908 steamboat **Sabino** makes trips *(30min)* on the river *(mid-May–mid-Oct daily 11am–4pm on the hour; $3.50; ♿).* Along the wharves and adjacent streets of the **waterfront** are businesses found in a 19C seaport, such as a printer, tavern, ship's chandlery and a ropewalk—the long cordage company building where rope necessary for rigging large vessels was made. Moored at the waterfront are the **Charles W. Morgan**, a survivor of America's 19C whaling fleet; the **Joseph Conrad**, a Danish-built training vessel (1882); and the **L.A. Dunton**, a schooner (1921) typical of fishing vessels that sailed to the Grand Banks off Newfoundland in the 1920s and 30s. At the **Henry B. du Pont Preservation Shipyard**, visitors may observe craftsmen restoring boats from the seaport's vast collection. The **Mystic River Scale Model** shows the village as it appeared in 1853. Enjoy the collections of **ship models** and **scrimshaw** in the Stillman Building and wooden **ship figureheads** in the Wendell Building.

Kitchen Little

81-1/2 Greenmanville Ave. ☎ 860-536-2122. Located near Mystic Seaport, this tiny, waterside eatery is well known for its huge and inventive breakfasts *(served 6:30am–2pm)* of pancakes, French toast, and egg dishes called the Mystic Melt, the Portuguese Fisherman or the Kitchen Sink. Lunch portions are hearty too. If indoor seating is unavailable, share a table outside with the seagulls.

★★**Mystic Aquarium** – Kids *55 Coogan Blvd. in Mystic. Open Jul–Labor Day daily 9am–6pm. Rest of the year daily 9am–5pm. Closed Jan 1, Thanksgiving Day, Dec 25. $15.* ✗ ♿ ☎ *860-572-5955. www.mysticaquarium.org.* Some 6,000 sea creatures live at this "institute for exploration." In the new **Ocean Planet Pavilion**, bonnethead sharks prowl a tank with exotic fish, while **Sunlit Seas** features species that thrive in ecosystems such as estuaries and coral reefs. Atlantic bottlenose dolphins play in the World of the Dolphin tank *(daily demonstrations)*. The **Challenge of the Deep** exhibit "submerges" visitors below the ocean surface to explore the diverse sea life.

Outside, penguins, sea lions and beluga whales can be found in settings resembling their natural habitats.

EXCURSION

★★**Mashantucket Pequot Museum** – Kids *7mi northeast of Mystic. From I-95, take exit 92, then Rte. 2 west and follow signs to museum. Open Memorial Day–Labor Day daily 10am–7pm. Rest of the year Wed–Mon 10am–6pm. Last admission 1 hr before closing. Closed Jan 1, Thanksgiving Day, Dec 25. $10.* ✗ ♿ ☎ *860-396-6800. www.mashantucket.com.* This tribally owned museum is devoted to the Mashantucket Pequots. Inside the glass and concrete facility (1998) that pays homage to nature, dioramas, videos, aromas and recorded sounds re-create day-to-day life from prehistoric times to the present. On level one, visitors pass through a simulated glacial crevasse of the ice age and a diorama of a caribou hunt. The highlight is the indoor 16C **Pequot Village**, a re-creation of a native dwelling site, complete with wigwams and cornfields. Level two is devoted to reservation life. Nearby is **Foxwoods Resort Casino**, also a Pequot enterprise.

Abbott's Lobster in the Rough

117 Pearl St., Noank (2.5mi southwest of Mystic via Rte. 215). ☎ *860-536-7719.* This rambling lobster shack is right on the waters of Fishers Island Sound. Dress casually and head for the outdoor menu to choose your lobster by weight. Or try the Hot Lobster Roll (1/4lb on a toasted bun) or the generous Seafood Feast (chowder, shrimp, steamers, mussels, lobster with slaw, chips and drawn butter). It's ok to bring your own beer or wine since alcoholic beverages are not served on the premises.

Randall's Ordinary

Rte. 2, North Stonington. ☎ *860-599-4540.* This country inn is situated on a 200-acre farm established in 1685. Prepared in an open hearth by costumed staff, the colonial prix-fixe fare is served with choice of scallops, duck or angus steak, for example. Shaker herb or butternut squash soup, bread baked in the beehive oven and vegetables accompany the entrée. From the tiny taproom, a barmaid serves Madeira wine, ale or cider. Apple crisp, or bread pudding based on a recipe said to be from Thomas Jefferson, completes the repast.

Index

Harkness Tower .... Building, street or other point of interest
Yale, Elihu .... Person, historic event or term
Sightseeing .... Practical information

A

B

C – D

E

F

G

H

K

L

M

N

O – P

Q – R

S

T

U

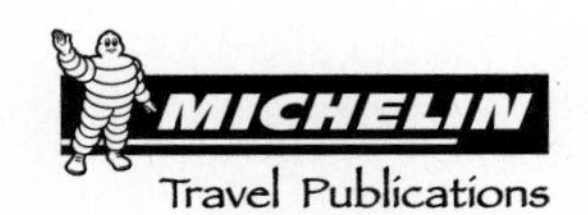

Michelin North America
One Parkway South, Greenville SC 29615, USA
Tel. 1-800-423-0485
www.michelin-travel.com

Manufacture Française des Pneumatiques Michelin
Société en commandite par actions au capital de 2 000 000 000 de francs
Place des Carmes-Déchaux – 63000 Clermont-Ferrand (France)
R.C.S. Clermont-Fd B 855 200 507

Michelin et Cie, Propriétaires-éditeurs, 2000
Dépôt légal avril 2000 – ISBN 2-06-155201-3 – ISSN 0763-1383

Printed in the EU 04-00/1/1

Compogravure : NORD COMPO, Villeneuve d'Ascq
Impression et brochage : AUBIN, Ligugé